MW01672320

STORIES IN TIME

INTERMEDIATE ATLAS

HARCOURT BRACE & COMPANY
Orlando Atlanta Austin Boston San Francisco Chicago Dallas
New York Toronto London

Photo Credits:
Key: (t) top; (b) bottom; (l) left; (r) right; (c) center

5 John Henley; 5 (insets) Harcourt Brace and Company/Victoria Bowen; 62 Roy Morsch/The Stock Market; 63 (l) The Bettmann Archive; 63 (r) Pete Saloutos/The Stock Market; 66 (l) Jonathan Nourok/PhotoEdit; 66 (inset) David Young-Wolff/PhotoEdit; 66 (r) John Elk III/Stock Boston; 67 (l) Chuck O'Rear/Westlight; 67 (c) Doris De Witt/Tony Stone Images; 67 (r) Douglas A. Faulkner/Photo Researchers; 70 (l) Culver Pictures; 70 (inset) Lawrence Migdale/Stock, Boston; 70 (c), 70(r) Missouri Historical Society; 71(l) The Kansas State Historical Society TOPEKA, KANSAS; 71 (r) The Granger Collection, New York; 74 (l) E.R. Degginger/Color-Pic; 74 (inset) Willard Clay/Tony Stone Images; 74 (r) Richard Pasley/Stock, Boston; 75 (l) Mark Burnett/Photo Researchers; 75 (r) Jim Pickerell/WestLight; 78 (tl), 78(bl) Harcourt Brace & Company/ Carroll Morgan; 78 (r) Greg Vaughan/Tom Stack & Associates; 79 (l) William S. Helsel/Tony Stone Images; 79 (c) Thomas H. Brakefield/ The Stock Market; 79 (r) Vince Streano/The Stock Market.

All maps by GeoSystems

Grateful acknowledgment is made to University of Missouri-Kansas City, University Libraries for permission to reprint "Maps" by Dorothy Brown Thompson.

Printed in the United States of America

ISBN 0-15-308473-1

1 2 3 4 5 6 7 8 9 10 085 99 98 97 96

CONTENTS

Maps

by Dorothy Brown Thompson

High adventure
  And bright dream—
Maps are mightier
  Than they seem:

Ships that follow
  Leaning stars—
Red and gold of
  Strange bazaars—

Ice floes hid
  Beyond all knowing—
Planes that ride where
  Winds are blowing!

Train maps, maps of
  Wind and weather,
Road maps—taken
  Altogether

Maps are really
  Magic wands
For home-staying
  Vagabonds!

S · K · I · L · L · S

How To

Read a Map

Why Is This Skill Important?

To answer questions about the world around you, you need information. You can get this information by reading this atlas, by looking at its pictures and charts, and by studying its maps. Maps tell you about the five themes of geography—location, place, human-environment interactions, movement, and regions. Knowing how to read maps is an important skill both for learning social studies and for taking action as a citizen.

The Parts of a Map

Most maps have several things in common. To help you read maps, mapmakers usually include a title, a key, a compass rose, a locator, and a scale on the maps they draw.

The map title tells you the subject of the map. Look the map below. What is the title of this map?

The map title may also help you understand what kind of map is shown. There are many kinds of maps. One kind is a physical map. It

shows mostly landforms and bodies of water. Another kind of map is a political map. It shows mostly cities and state or national boundaries. **Boundary** is another word for *border,* or the outside edge of a place. What two countries share a national border with the United States?

⊛ National capital
★ State capital
— National border
— State border

The **map key**, which is sometimes called a map legend, explains what the symbols on the map stand for. A **symbol** is something that stands for something else. On a map, a symbol represents a real object in the world. Symbols on maps may be colors, patterns, lines, or other special marks. On the map on page 6, a dot is used to show a city. What symbol is used to show a state capital? What symbol is used to show the national capital?

The **compass rose**, or direction marker on a map, shows the main directions, or cardinal directions. The **cardinal directions** are north, south, east, and west. The compass rose also helps you find the **intermediate directions**, or the directions between the cardinal directions. Intermediate directions are northeast, southeast, southwest, and northwest.

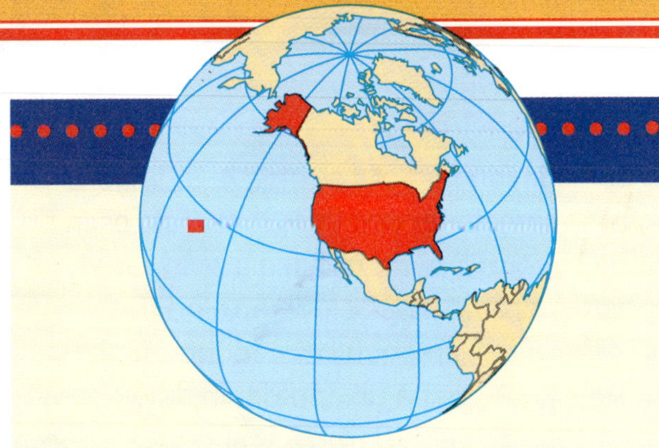

The **locator** is a small map or globe that shows where the place on the main map is located in a state, in a country, or in the world. The locator on the map of the United States is a globe that shows North America. The United States is shown in red.

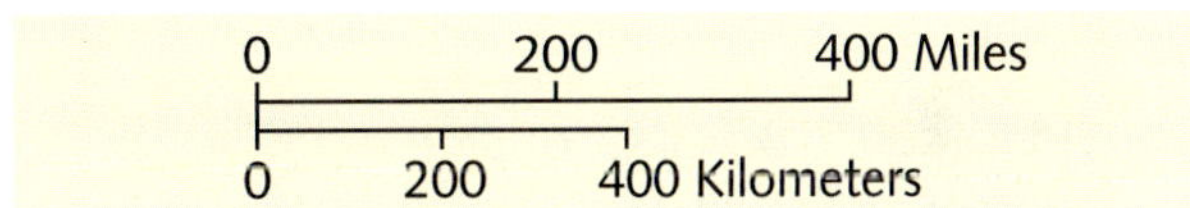

The **map scale** compares a distance on a map with a distance in the real world. A map scale helps you find the real distance between places on a map. Each map in this atlas has a scale that shows both miles and kilometers.

Find Alaska and Hawaii on the map of the United States. These states are not shown where they really are. Hundreds of miles separate them from the other 48 states. To show the whole area between Alaska, Hawaii, and the other states, the map would have to be much larger, or each part of the map would have to be much smaller. Instead, Alaska and Hawaii are each shown in an **inset map**, or a small map within a larger map. The boxes around Alaska and Hawaii show that they are inset maps.

An inset map often has its own map scale. Look at Alaska on the map of the United States. On the Earth, Alaska is more than twice the size of Texas, but on the map, Alaska is much smaller than Texas. This is because the scales on the inset map and the main map are different.

Understand the Process

To help you find places on a map, mapmakers sometimes add lines that cross each other to form a pattern called a **grid**. Study the map of Arkansas below. Around the grid are letters and numbers. In this grid the columns, which run up and down, have numbers. The rows, which run left and right, have letters. Each square on the map can be identified by its letter and number.

A map with a grid may have an index such as the one you see beside this map. The index helps you find the names of the places you are looking for. It lists them in alphabetical order. The index also gives the grid letter and number for each place.

1. Find Little Rock, Arkansas's capital, in the map index. What are Little Rock's grid letter and number?
2. Find the letter *B* and the number *2* on the grid. Put a finger of one hand on the letter *B* and a finger of your other hand on the number *2*. Move your fingers toward each other, along row B and column 2. You will find Little Rock in the square where your fingers meet.
3. Now find Fayetteville on the map. In what square is it located? In what square is the city of Fort Smith located?
4. What city is located in square *C-3?* Check your answer with the map index.

Think and Apply

Look at the map of Arkansas again. Identify the parts of the map, and discuss with a partner what the map tells you about the state. Then take turns using the map grid to find different places in the state.

ARKANSAS

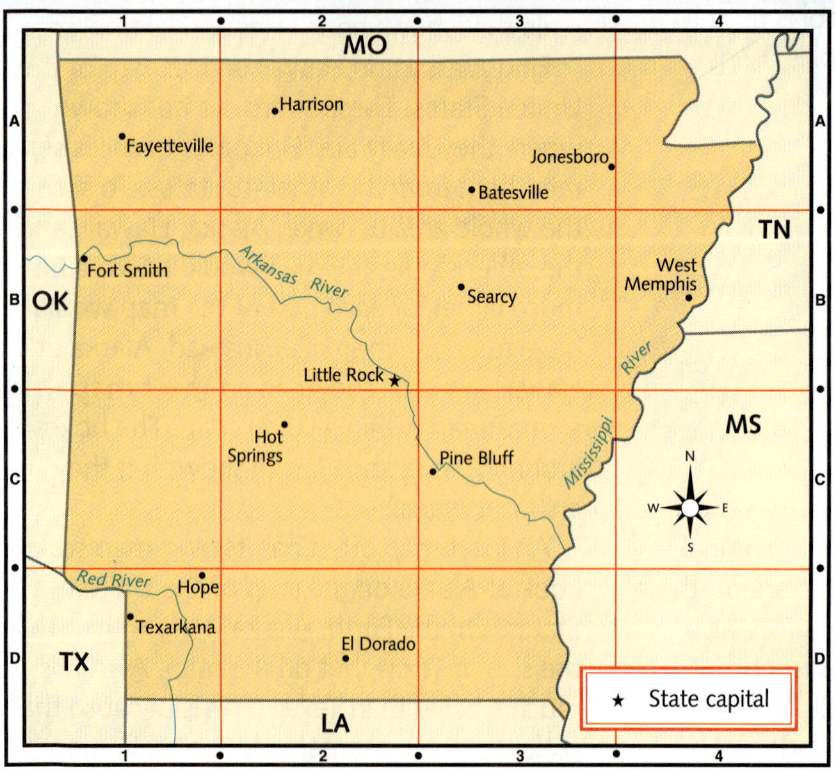

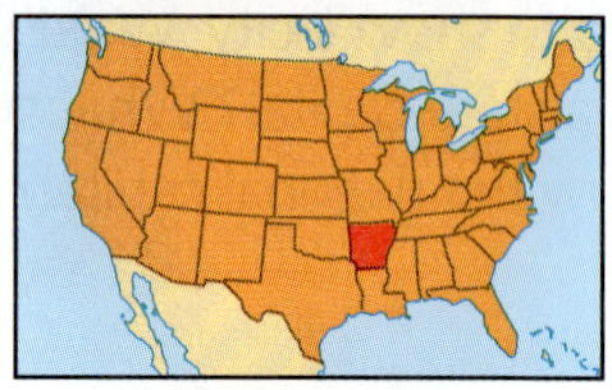

Index to Cities

Batesville..........A-3
El Dorado..........D-2
Fayetteville........A-1
Fort Smith..........B-1
Harrison............A-2
Hope.................D-1
Hot Springs........C-2
Jonesboro..........A-3
Little Rock..........B-2
Pine Bluff...........C-3
Searcy...............B-3
Texarkana..........D-1
West Memphis...B-4

0 40 80 Miles
0 40 80 Kilometers
Albers Equal-Area Projection

S•K•I•L•L•S

How To

Use Latitude and Longitude

Why Is This Skill Important?

Just as the numbers of your home address describe where you live in your town, the numbers of your global address tell where your town is located on the Earth. The numbers in a global address stand for lines of latitude and lines of longitude. You can use these lines to help you describe the absolute, or exact, location of any place on the Earth.

Lines of Latitude

Mapmakers use a system of imaginary lines to form a grid on maps and globes. The lines that run east and west are the **lines of latitude**. Lines of latitude are also called **parallels** (PAIR•uh•lelz). This is because they are parallel, or always the same distance from each other. Parallel lines never meet.

Lines of latitude are measured in degrees north and south from the equator, which is labeled 0°, or *zero degrees.* The parallels north of the equator are marked *N* for *north latitude*. This means they are in the Northern Hemisphere. The parallels south of the equator are marked *S* for *south latitude*. This means they are in the Southern Hemisphere. The greater the number of degrees marking a parallel, the farther north or south of the equator it is.

Lines of Longitude

The lines that run north and south on a map are the **lines of longitude**, or **meridians**. Each meridian runs from the North Pole to the South Pole. Unlike parallels, which never meet, meridians meet at the poles. Meridians are farthest apart at the equator.

Meridians are numbered in much the same way as parallels are numbered. The meridian marked 0° is called the **prime meridian**. It runs north and south through Greenwich, near the

LINES OF LATITUDE

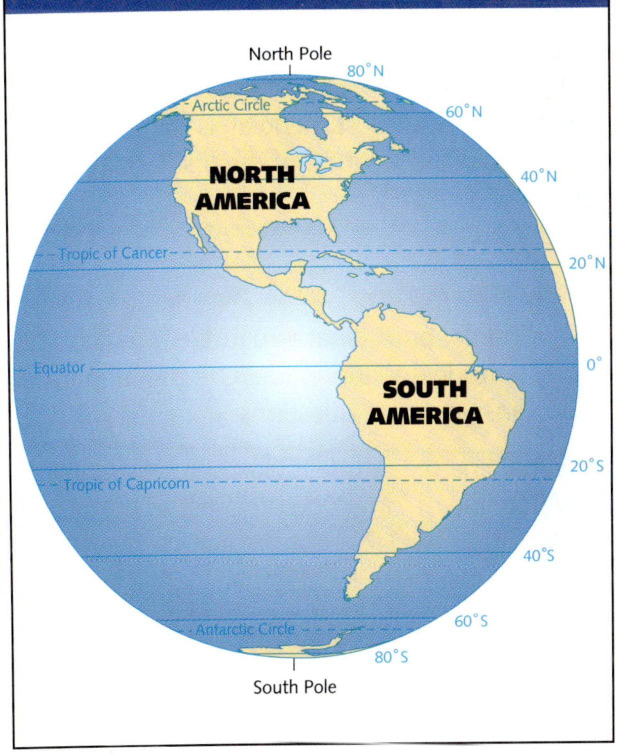

LINES OF LONGITUDE

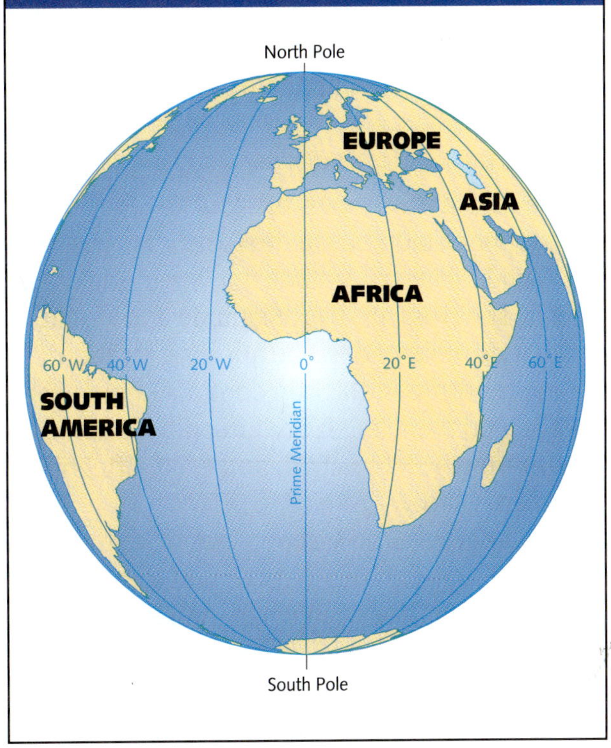

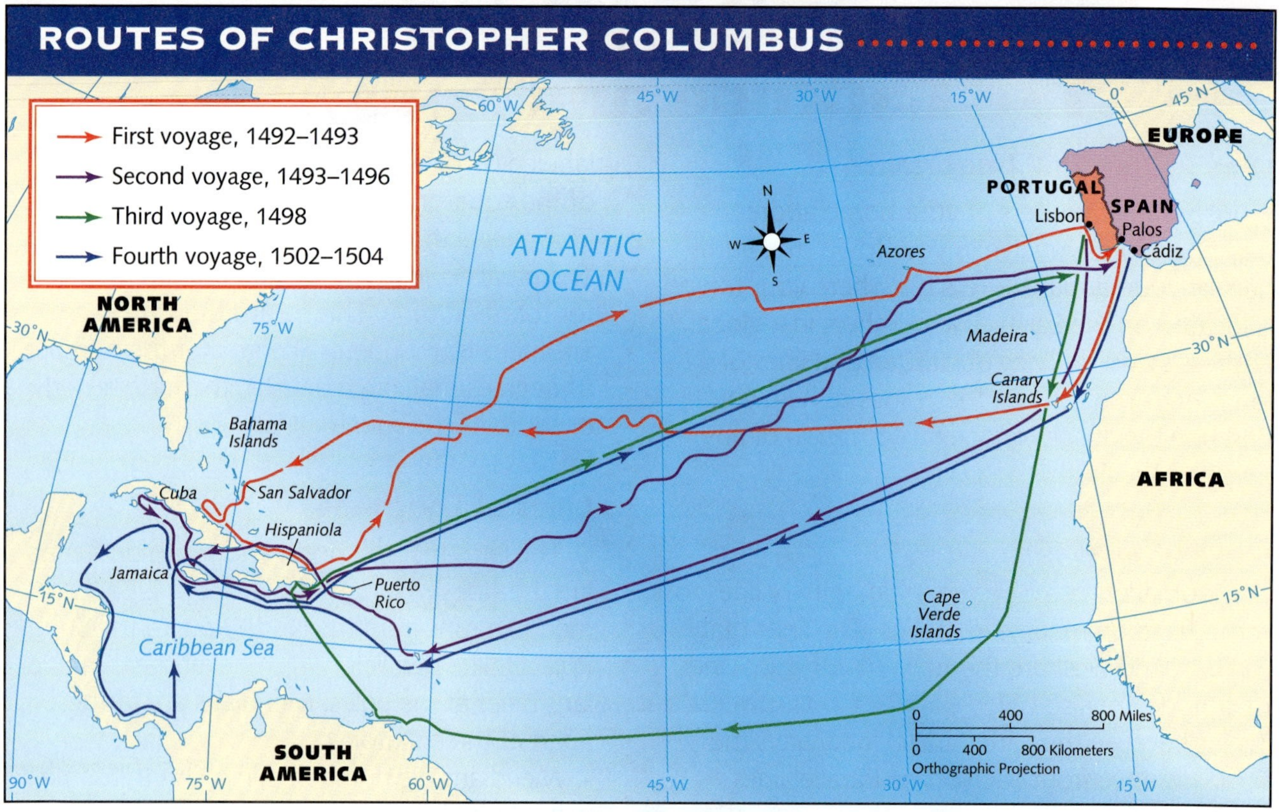

city of London in Britain. Lines of longitude to the west of the prime meridian are marked *W* for *west longitude*. They are in the Western Hemisphere. The meridians to the east of prime meridian are marked *E* for *east longitude*. They are in the Eastern Hemisphere.

Understand the Process

The map above shows the four voyages of Christopher Columbus to the Americas. The map has a grid of lines of latitude and longitude drawn over it. The crossing lines of latitude and longitude make it possible to describe absolute location.

Like most maps, this one does not show every parallel and meridian. Every fifteenth parallel is shown from 15°N to 45°N, and every fifteenth meridian is shown from 0° to 90°W.

Now that you know about lines of latitude and longitude, you can use them to find some locations. At either side of the map, find 30°N. At the top or bottom, find 15°W. Use a finger of each hand to trace these lines to the point where they cross each other. The Canary Islands are not far from this point. So you can say that the location of the Canary Islands is near 30°N, 15°W.

Look for the latitude and longitude that describe the location of Columbus's first landing in the Americas. The closest parallels are 15°N and 30°N. The closest meridian is 75°W. So you can say that the location of the first landing is about 22°N, 75°W.

Think and Apply

Map Skill

Think about what you just learned about latitude and longitude. Use the map to answer these questions.

1. What line of latitude is closest to Hispaniola?
2. What line of longitude is closest to the Bahama Islands?
3. What islands are located near 15°N, 30°W?
4. Which location is farther north, 45°N, 60°W or 30°N, 90°W?
5. Which location is farther east, 45°N, 60°W or 30°N, 90°W?

Compare Maps with Different Projections

Why Is This Skill Important?

Over the centuries Arab, Chinese, and European mapmakers have developed different ways to show the round Earth in the form of a flat map. These different representations of the Earth are called **projections**. Every map projection has **distortions**, or parts that are not accurate. This is because the shape of the round Earth needs to be split or stretched to make it flat. Identifying these distortions will help you understand how map projections can best be used.

Map Projections and Their Uses

Different kinds of map projections have different kinds of distortions. Some map projections distort the shape or the size of the area shown. Some show distances to be greater or less than they actually are. One way that mapmakers classify map projections is by the properties that are distorted the least.

Map A is an equal-area projection. Notice that the prime meridian and the equator divide the hemispheres so that their areas are equal. An **equal-area projection** shows the sizes of regions in correct relation to one another, but it distorts shapes. Because an equal-area projection shows correct size relations of regions, it is useful for comparing information about different parts of the world. The projection on Map A below is just one of the many different kinds of equal-area projections.

Map B is a conformal projection. Notice that the lines of longitude are all an equal distance apart. On a globe the lines of longitude get closer together as they near the poles, where they meet. Also notice on Map B that the lines of latitude closer to the poles are farther apart.

MAP A: EQUAL-AREA PROJECTION

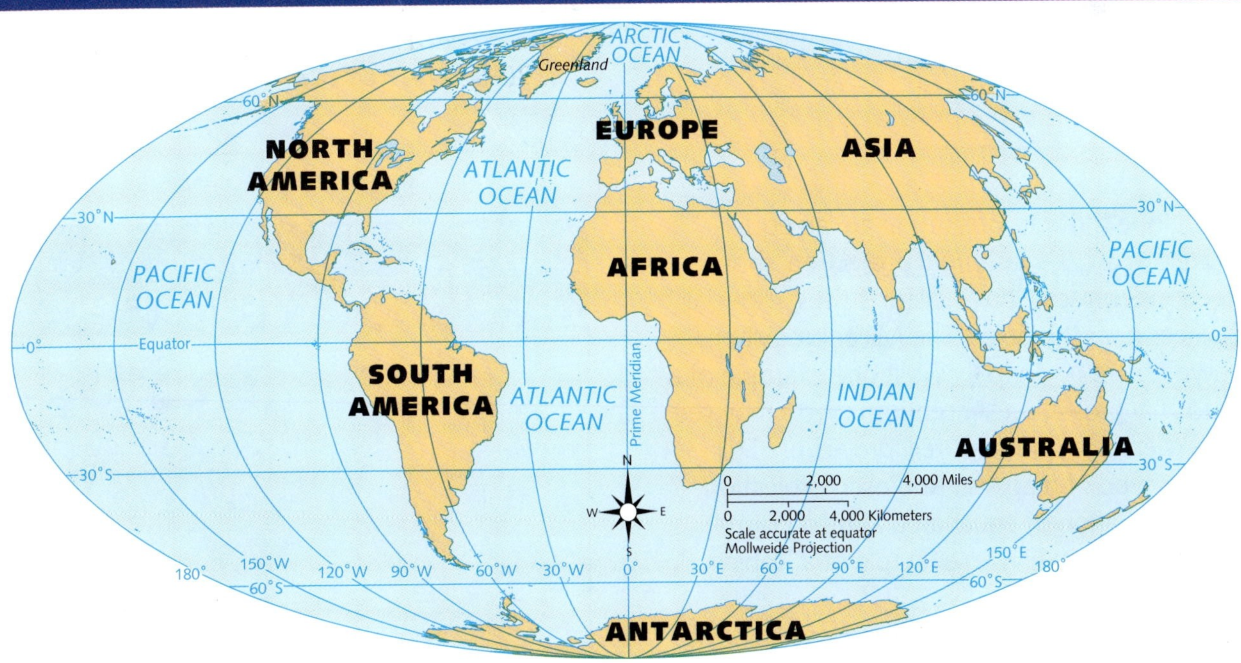

MAP B: CONFORMAL PROJECTION

On a globe the lines of latitude are an equal distance apart. A **conformal projection** shows directions correctly, but it distorts sizes, especially of places near the poles. The Miller projection, shown above on Map B, is just one example of a conformal projection. Another that you may see is the Mercator (mer•KAY•ter) projection. Still another type of map, the Robinson projection, is a combination of equal-area and conformal projections. Map C is an example of a Robinson projection.

Map D is an **equidistant projection**. It shows accurate distances from a central point. Any

MAP C: ROBINSON PROJECTION

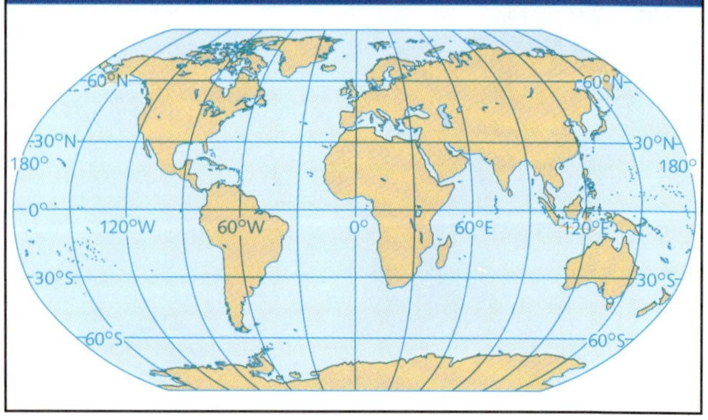

MAP D: EQUIDISTANT PROJECTION

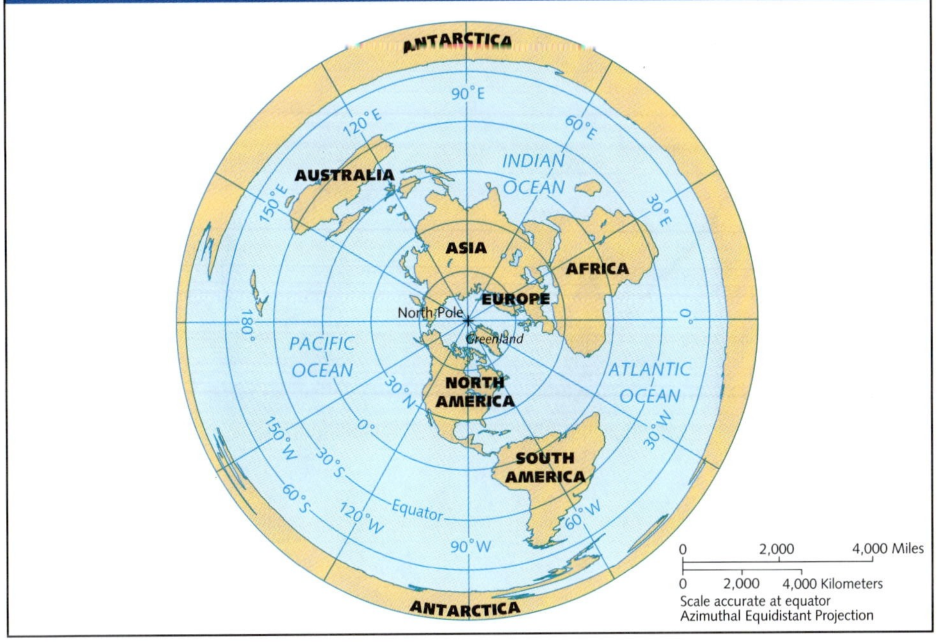

place on the Earth can be chosen as the central point. Often the central point chosen is one of the poles. That kind of map is called a **polar projection**. Either the North Pole or the South Pole can be the center of a polar projection. Notice on Map D that the North Pole is at the center of the map. The lines of latitude are circles, and the circles farther from the center are larger. Lines of longitude on Map D are straight lines that extend from the center in all directions, like the spokes of a wheel.

A **great circle** is any imaginary circle that divides the Earth into equal parts. The equator is a great circle. Lines of longitude are great circles, too. Because the Earth's surface is curved, the shortest distance between any two places is not really a straight line but part of a great circle. An equidistant projection is useful for finding the distance from the central point to other places on the map. Another projection, the gnomonic projection, is also important when studying great circle routes. In this projection all straight lines are great circle routes. Therefore, these lines show the shortest routes between two places. Distances on this projection are not accurate, however.

Understand the Process

Compare and contrast Maps A, B, C, and D by answering the questions below. As you answer the questions, think about the advantages and disadvantages of each map projection.

1. South America is much larger than Greenland. Which projection shows Greenland's size more accurately, Map A or Map B?
2. The greatest east-west distance in Africa is about the same as the greatest north-south distance. Which projection shows Africa's shape more accurately, Map A or Map B?
3. The North Pole is a single point. Which projections show the North Pole accurately?
4. Which map can be called a polar projection?
5. On which map do the lines of longitude get closer together toward both poles?
6. On which map or maps are the lines of longitude parallel, or equally far apart?

Think and Apply

Map Skill

Write a paragraph about the advantages and disadvantages of using each kind of map.

basin bowl-shaped area of land surrounded by higher land

bay body of water that is part of a sea or ocean and is partly enclosed by land

bluff high, steep face of rock or earth

canyon deep, narrow valley with steep sides

cape a point of land that extends into water

cataract large waterfall

cliff high, steep face of rock or earth

coast land along a sea or ocean

coastal plain area of flat land along a sea or ocean

delta triangle-shaped area of land at the mouth of a river

desert dry land with few plants

dune hill of sand piled up by the wind

fall line area along which rivers form waterfalls or rapids as the rivers drop to lower land

fjord deep, narrow part of a sea or ocean, between high, steep banks

floodplain flat land that is near the edges of a river and is formed by the silt deposited by floods

foothills hilly area at the base of a mountain

glacier large ice mass that moves slowly down a mountain or across land

gulf body of water that is partly enclosed by land but is larger than a bay

hill land that rises above the land around it

island land that has water on all sides

isthmus narrow strip of land connecting two larger areas of land

lagoon body of shallow water

lake body of water with land on all sides

marsh lowland with moist soil and tall grasses

mesa flat-topped mountain with steep sides

mountain highest kind of land

mountain pass gap between mountains

mountain range row of mountains

mouth of river place where a river empties into another body of water

oasis area of water and fertile land with desert on all sides

ocean body of salt water, larger than a sea

peak top of a mountain

peninsula land that is almost completely surrounded by water

plain flat land

plateau area of high, flat land with steep sides

reef ridge of sand, rock, or coral that lies at or near the surface of a sea or ocean

river large stream of water that flows across the land

riverbank land along a river

savanna large area of grassland containing scattered trees

sea body of salt water, smaller than an ocean

sea level the level that is even with the surface of an ocean or sea

source of river place where a river or stream begins

strait narrow channel of water connecting two larger bodies of water

swamp area of low, wet land with trees

timberline line on a mountain above which it is too cold for trees to grow

tributary stream or river that empties into a larger river

valley low land between hills or mountains

volcano opening in the Earth, often raised, through which lava, rock, ashes, and gases are forced out

THE WORLD

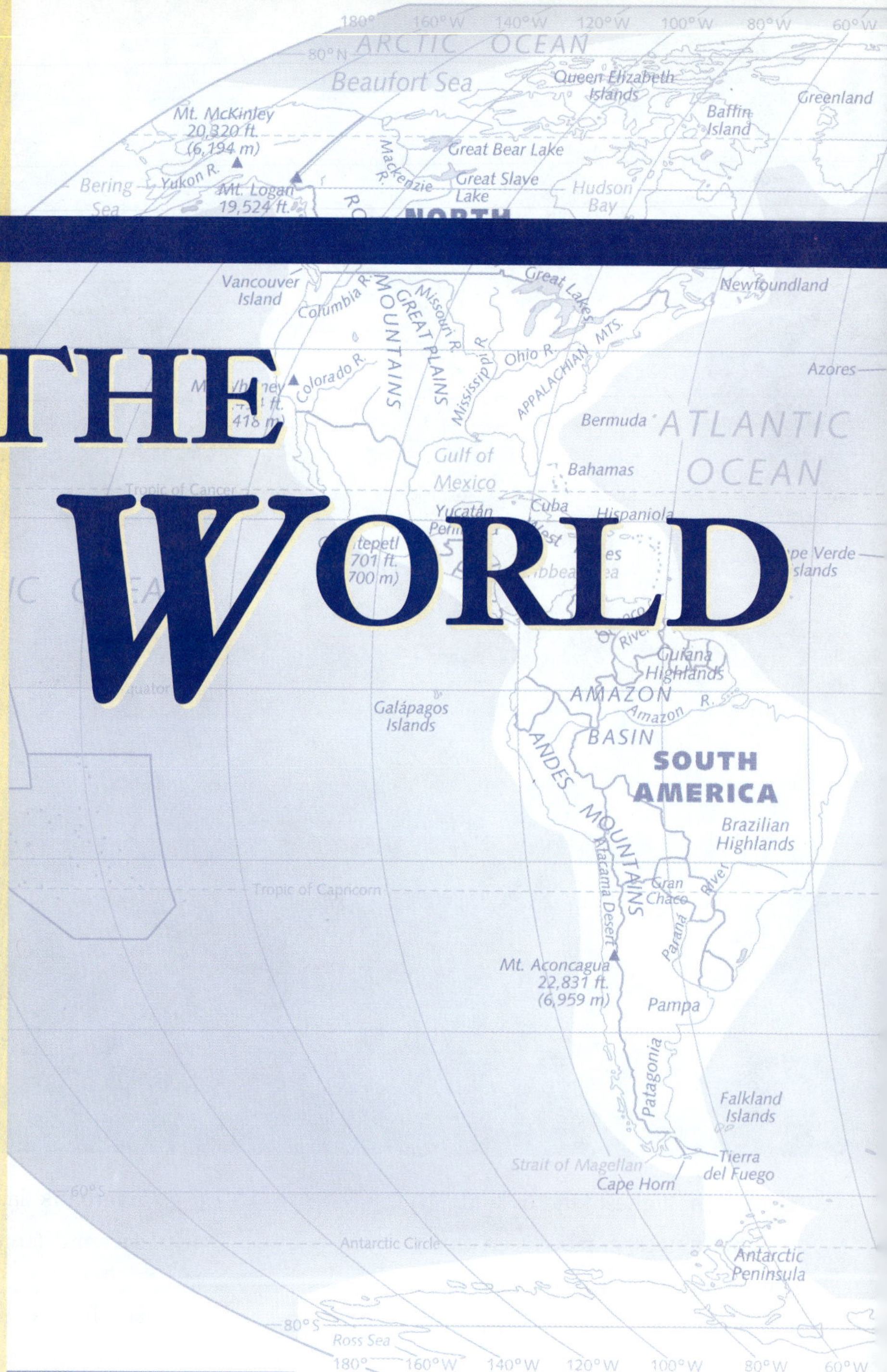
ARCTIC OCEAN
Beaufort Sea
Queen Elizabeth Islands
Greenland
Baffin Island
Mt. McKinley 20,320 ft. (6,194 m)
Great Bear Lake
Great Slave Lake
Hudson Bay
Bering Sea
Yukon R.
Mt. Logan 19,524 ft.
Vancouver Island
Newfoundland
Columbia R.
GREAT PLAINS
Missouri R.
Mississippi R.
Ohio R.
APPALACHIAN MTS.
Great Lakes
Colorado R.
Azores
Bermuda
ATLANTIC OCEAN
Gulf of Mexico
Bahamas
Cuba
Hispaniola
Tropic of Cancer
Galápagos Islands
Guiana Highlands
AMAZON BASIN
Amazon R.
ANDES MOUNTAINS
SOUTH AMERICA
Brazilian Highlands
Atacama Desert
Gran Chaco
Paraná River
Tropic of Capricorn
Mt. Aconcagua 22,831 ft. (6,959 m)
Pampa
Patagonia
Falkland Islands
Strait of Magellan
Cape Horn
Tierra del Fuego
Antarctic Circle
Antarctic Peninsula
Ross Sea
180° 160°W 140°W 120°W 100°W 80°W 60°W

EUROPE
Baltic Sea
Norwegian Sea
North Sea
British Isles
Iceland
ATLANTIC OCEAN
Arctic Circle

THE WORLD: POLITICAL

CENTRAL AMERICA AND THE CARIBBEAN

National border

Abbreviations

EQU. GUINEA	EQUATORIAL GUINEA
NETH.	NETHERLANDS
N.Z.	NEW ZEALAND
U.A.E.	UNITED ARAB EMIRATES
U.K.	UNITED KINGDOM
U.S.	UNITED STATES

THE WORLD: PHYSICAL

NORTHERN POLAR REGION

SOUTHERN POLAR REGION

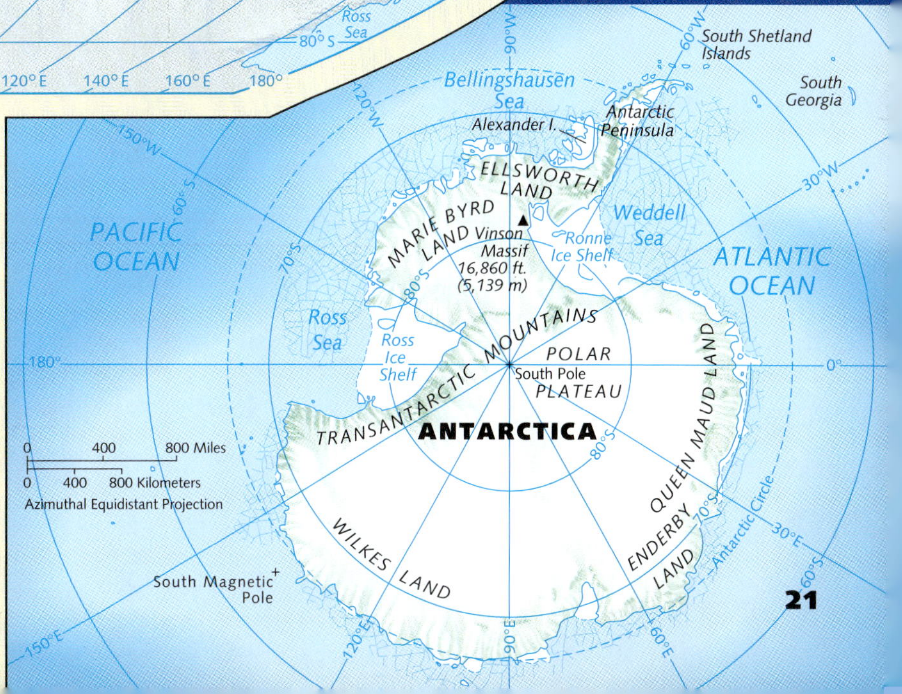

AFRICA: POLITICAL

AFRICA: PHYSICAL

EUROPE AND ASIA: POLITICAL

Abbreviations

AUST.	AUSTRIA
BELG.	BELGIUM
BOS. & HERZ.	BOSNIA AND HERZEGOVINA
CRO.	CROATIA
LIECHT.	LIECHTENSTEIN
LUX.	LUXEMBOURG
MAC.	MACEDONIA
NETH.	NETHERLANDS
PORT.	PORTUGAL
SLOV.	SLOVENIA
SWITZ.	SWITZERLAND
U.K.	UNITED KINGDOM
U.S.	UNITED STATES
YUGO.	YUGOSLAVIA

Severnaya Zemlya
Laptev Sea
New Siberian Islands
East Siberian Sea
Wrangel I.
ALASKA (U.S.)
Arctic Circle
Bering Strait
RUSSIA
Yenisey River
Angara River
Lena River
Magadan
Bering Sea
Krasnoyarsk
Novosibirsk
Lake Baikal
Irkutsk
Sea of Okhotsk
Petropavlovsk-Kamchatskiy
Sakhalin
Khabarovsk
MONGOLIA
Ulaanbaatar
Kuril Islands
Harbin
Sapporo
Vladivostok
Ürümqi
Changchun
Shenyang
NORTH KOREA
Sea of Japan
Beijing
Tianjin
P'yongyang
Taiyuan
Seoul
SOUTH KOREA
JAPAN
Tokyo
Yokohama
Nagoya
Osaka
Pusan
Yellow Sea
Huang He
Xian
CHINA
Chengdu
Nanjing
Shanghai
Wuhan
Lhasa
Chongqing
Chang Jiang
East China Sea
Ryukyu Islands
Okinawa
Kathmandu
NEPAL
Thimphu
BHUTAN
PACIFIC OCEAN
Kunming
Taipei
TAIWAN
BANGLADESH
Dhaka
Tropic of Cancer
Guangzhou
Chittagong
Calcutta
BURMA (MYANMAR)
Hanoi
Macao (PORT.)
Hong Kong
LAOS
Hainan
Bay of Bengal
Chiang Mai
Vientiane
Mekong R.
Hue
South China Sea
Philippine Sea
Rangoon (Yangon)
THAILAND
Quezon City
Manila
Bangkok
VIETNAM
CAMBODIA
PHILIPPINES
Andaman Islands (INDIA)
Phnom Penh
Ho Chi Minh City
Sulu Sea
Davao
Nicobar Islands (INDIA)
Bandar Seri Begawan
BRUNEI
Kuala Lumpur
MALAYSIA
Celebes Sea
Medan
SINGAPORE
Singapore
Halmahera
Equator
Borneo
Sumatra
Celebes
New Guinea
INDONESIA
Java Sea
Banda Sea
Jakarta
Bandung
Java
Surabaya
Arafura Sea
Timor
Timor Sea
AUSTRALIA
75° N
60° N
45° N
30° N
15° N
0°
15° S
90° E
105° E
120° E
135° E
150° E
165° E
180°
165° W

EUROPE AND ASIA: PHYSICAL

ARCTIC OCEAN
Laptev Sea
New Siberian Islands
East Siberian Sea
Taimyr Peninsula
Wrangel Island
Chukchi Sea
Bering Strait
Arctic Circle
Chukchi Peninsula
North Siberian Lowland
Central Siberian Plateau
Kolyma Lowland
Verkhoyansk Range
Kolyma R.
Kolyma Mountains
Korya Range
Yenisey River
SIBERIA
Lena River
Angara River
Bering Sea
Dzhugdzhur Range
Stanovoy Range
Kamchatka Peninsula
Central Range
Sea of Okhotsk
Lake Baikal
Sayan Mountains
Yenisey R.
Yablonovyy Range
Sakhalin
Greater Khingan Range
Amur River
Sikhote Alin Range
Kuril Islands
Altai Mountains
Junggar Basin
Plateau of Mongolia
Manchurian Plain
Hokkaido
Turpan Depression
-505 ft.
(-154 m)
Gobi (Desert)
Sea of Japan
Qilian Shan
Korean Peninsula
North China Plain
Huang He
Yellow Sea
Honshu
Mt. Fuji
12,388 ft.
(3,776 m)
Plateau of Tibet
Kyushu
Shikoku
Sichuan Basin
Chiang Jiang
East China Sea
Mt. Everest
29,028 ft.
(8,848 m)
Kanchenjunga
28,208 ft.
(8,598 m)
PACIFIC OCEAN
Ryukyu Islands
Ganges R.
Irrawaddy River
Tropic of Cancer
Taiwan
Philippine Sea
Gulf of Tonkin
Hainan
Mekong R.
Bay of Bengal
Khorat Plateau
South China Sea
Luzon
Indochina Peninsula
Andaman Islands
Philippine Islands
Andaman Sea
Gulf of Thailand
Palawan
Sulu Sea
Nicobar Islands
Mindanao
Malay Peninsula
Celebes Sea
Strait of Malacca
Halmahera
Borneo
0° Equator
Sumatra
Moluccas
Celebes
Rantekombola
11,335 ft.
(3,455 m)
Ceram
Greater Sunda Islands
Java Sea
New Guinea
Banda Sea
Java
Bali
Sumbawa
Lesser Sunda Islands
Flores
Timor
Lombok
Sumba
Timor Sea
Arafura Sea
AUSTRALIA

THE WESTERN HEMISPHERE: POLITICAL

THE WESTERN HEMISPHERE: PHYSICAL

THE PACIFIC RIM: POLITICAL AND PHYSICAL

MAJOR RIVERS OF THE WORLD

THE WORLD'S MAJOR RIVERS

RIVER	LENGTH		CONTINENT
	in miles	in kilometers	
Nile	4,187	6,738	Africa
Amazon	4,000	6,437	South America
Chang Jiang	3,434	5,526	Asia
Mississippi	2,348	3,779	North America
Volga	2,293	3,690	Europe
Darling	1,702	2,739	Australia
Ganges	1,557	2,506	Asia
Rhine	820	1,320	Europe

MOUNTAINS OF THE WORLD

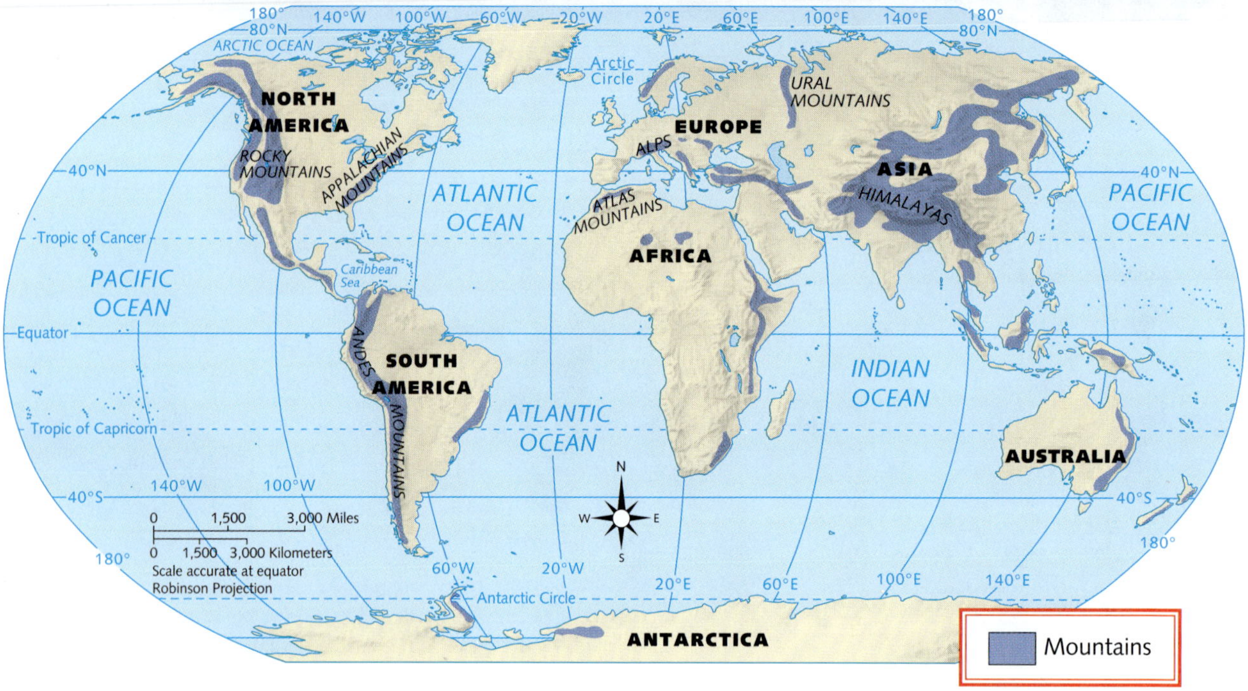

HIGHEST MOUNTAIN ON EACH CONTINENT

MAJOR PLAINS OF THE WORLD

MAJOR DESERTS OF THE WORLD

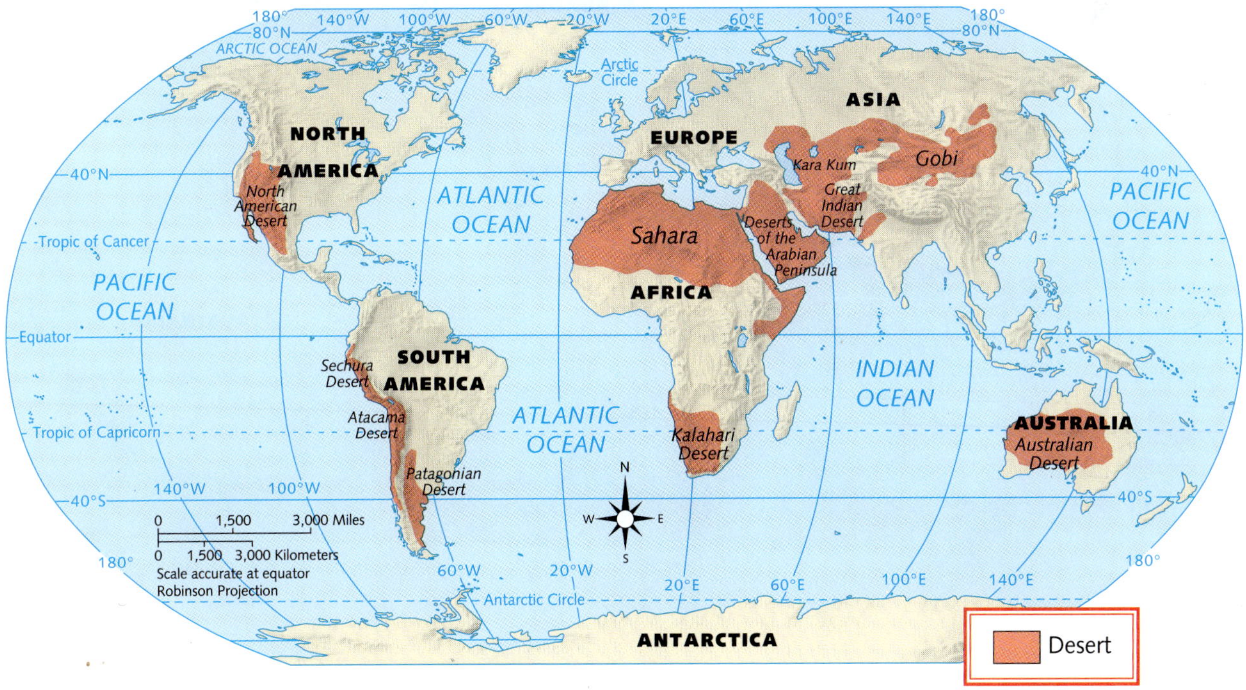

MIGRATION OF EARLY PEOPLE

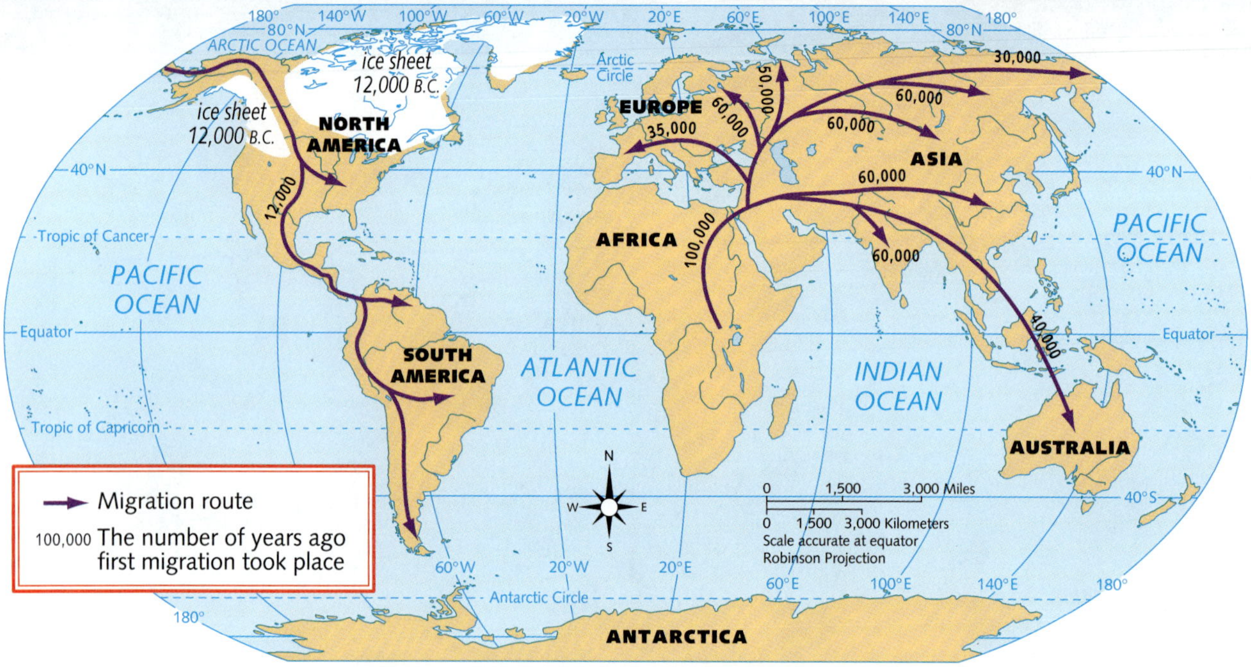

EARLY FARMING AREAS

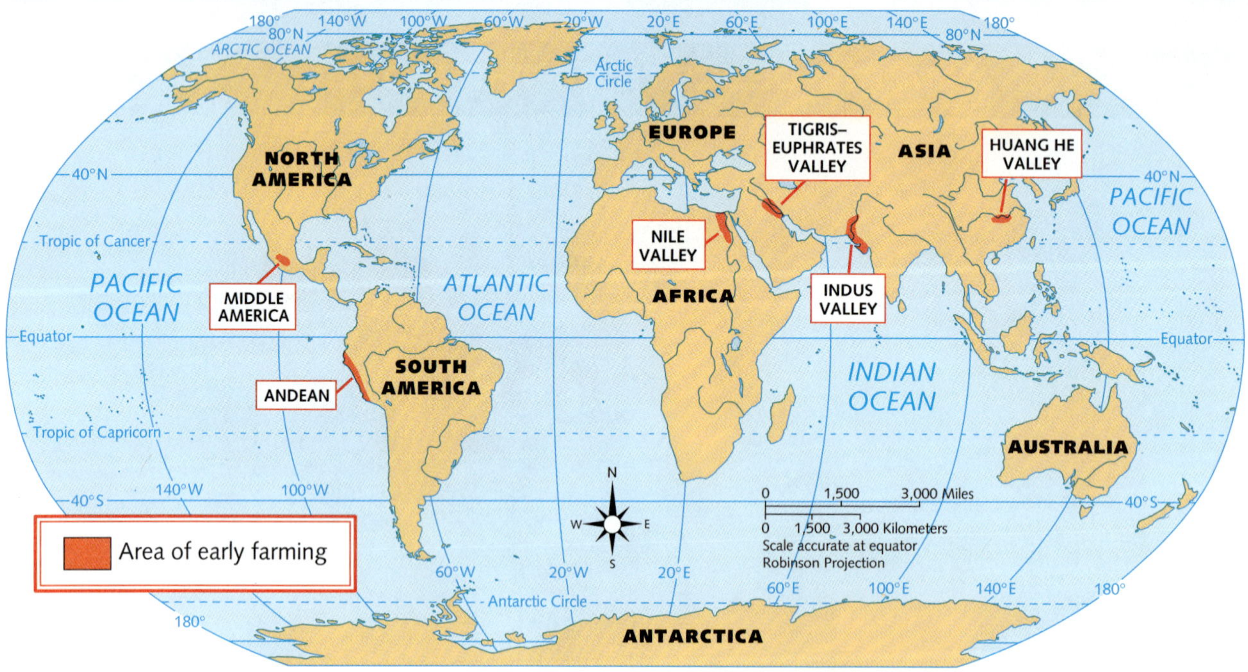

MAJOR CITIES OF THE 1400s

VOYAGES OF EXPLORATION

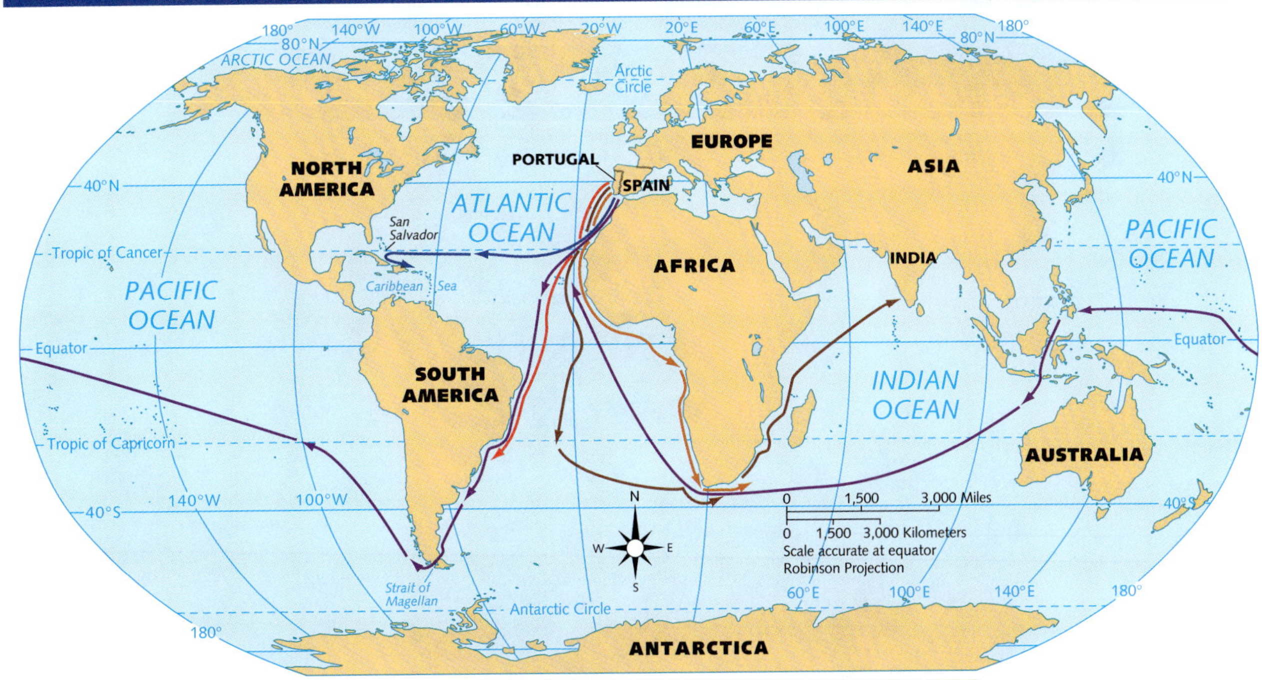

Spanish explorers
- Columbus, 1492–1493
- Magellan, 1519–1522

Portugese explorers
- Dias, 1487–1488
- Da Gama, 1497–1499
- Vespucci, 1501

WORLD LANGUAGES

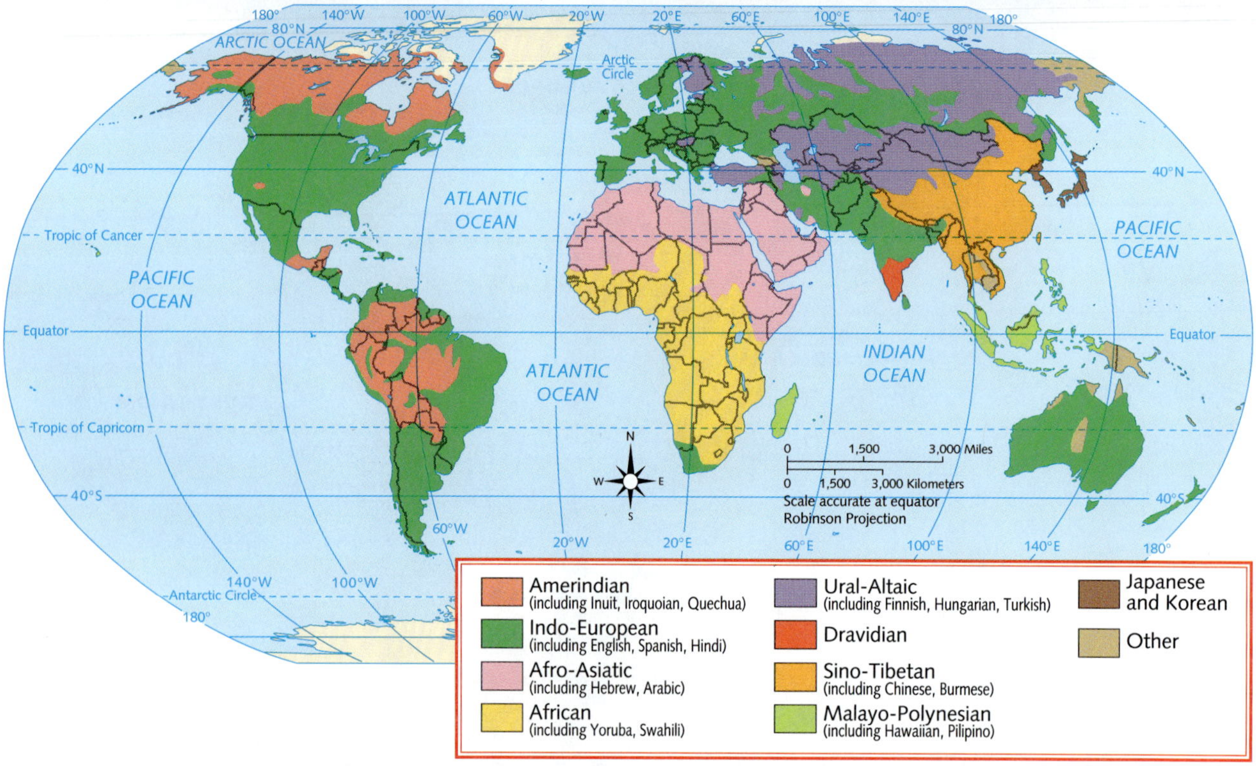

WORLD RELIGIONS

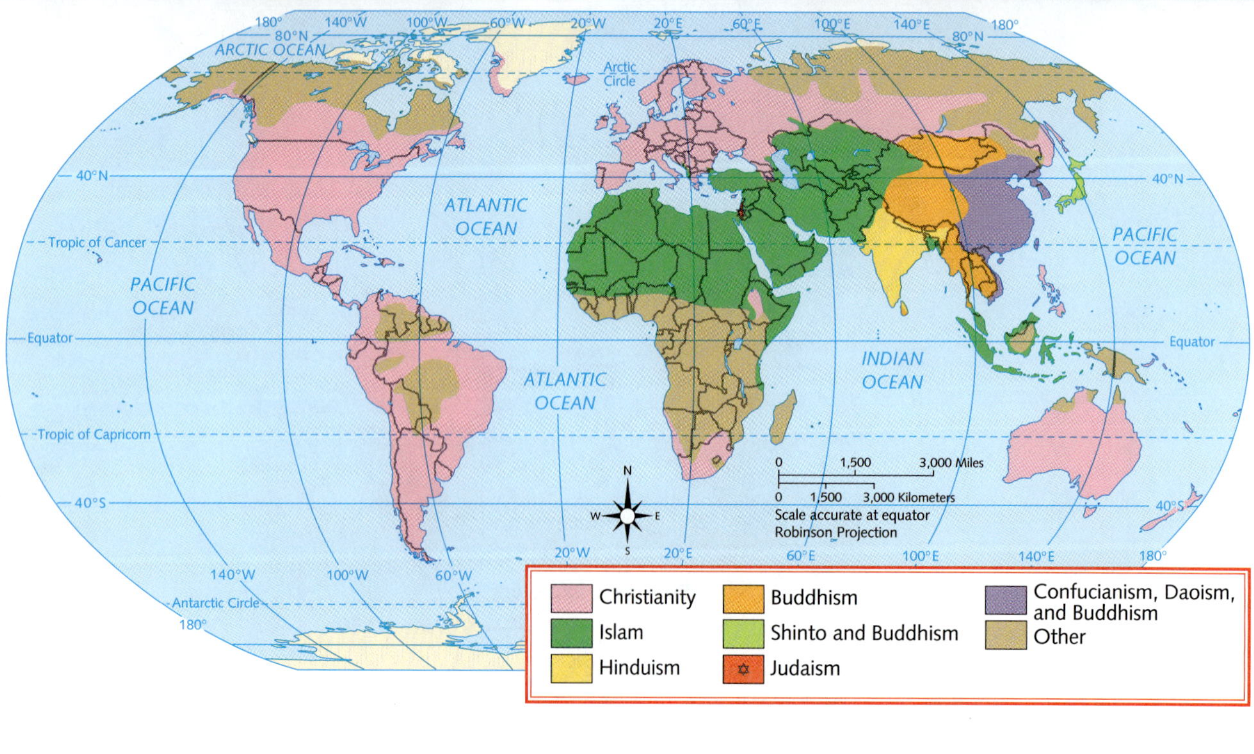

TIME ZONES OF THE WORLD

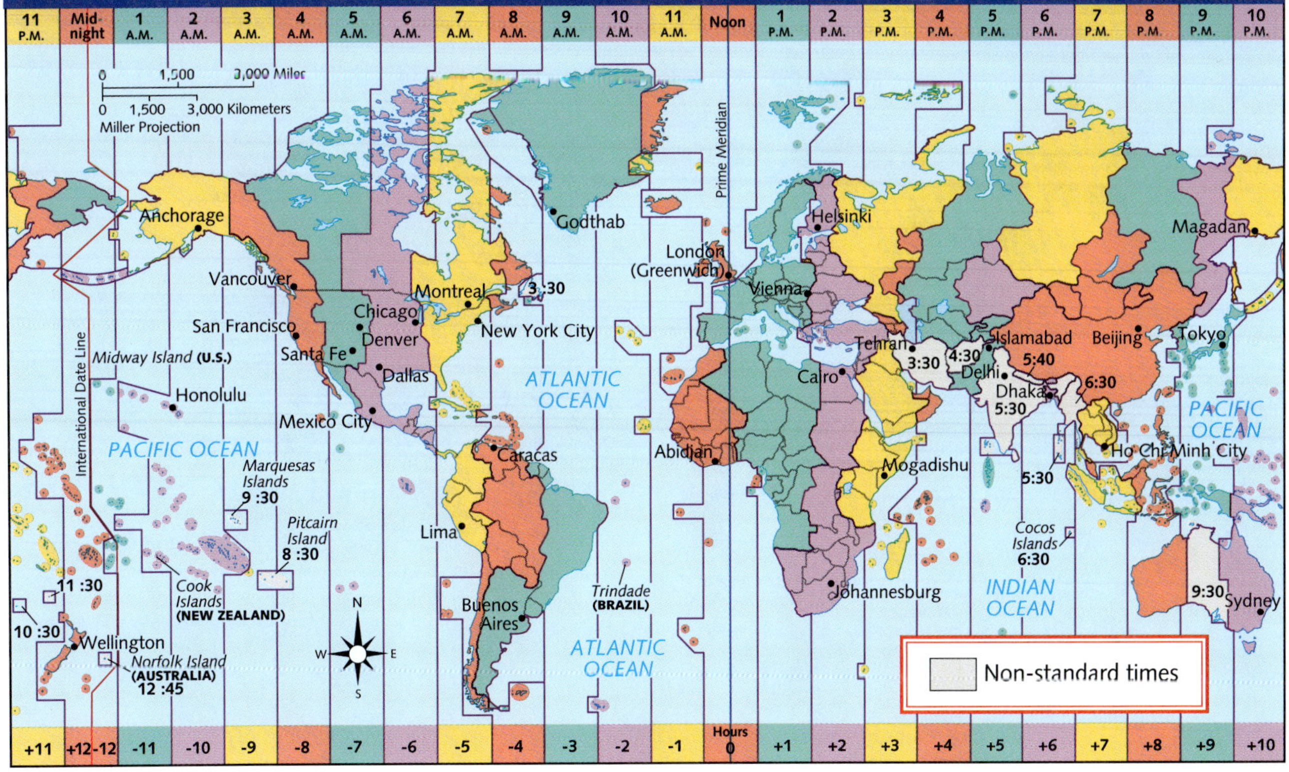

CLOCKS AROUND THE WORLD

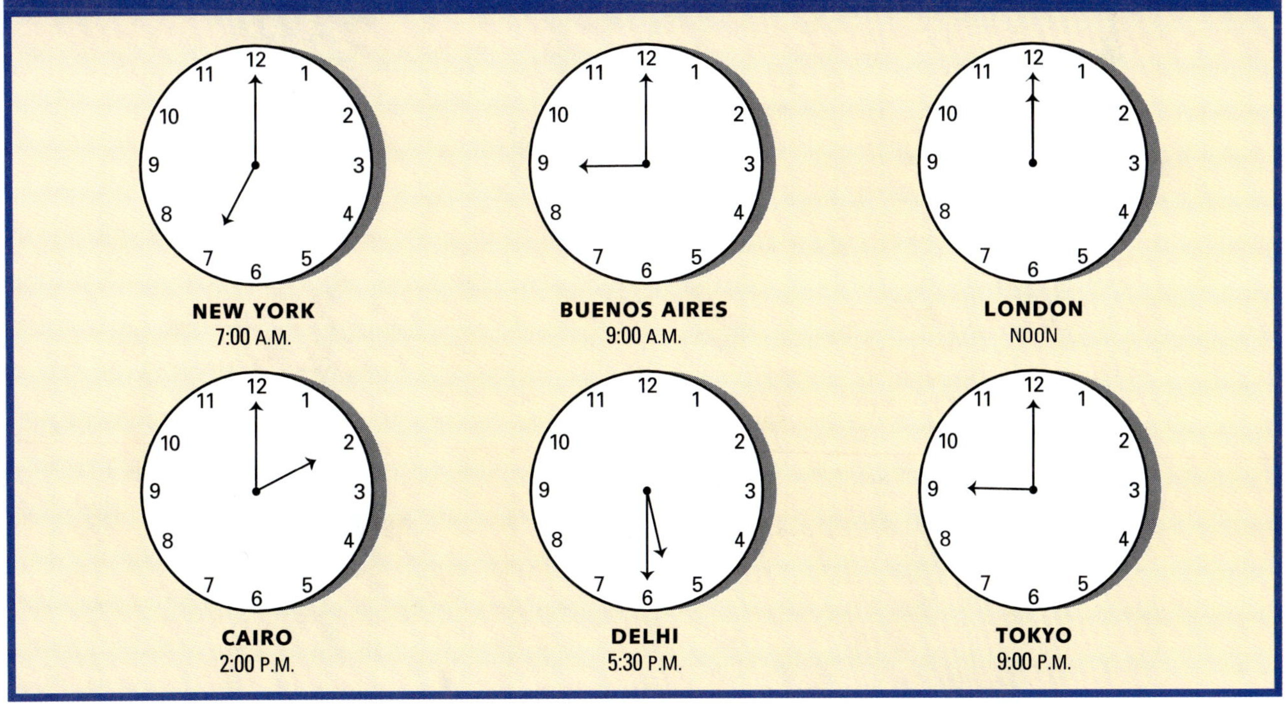

POLITICAL MAP OF THE WORLD

WORLD POPULATION CARTOGRAM

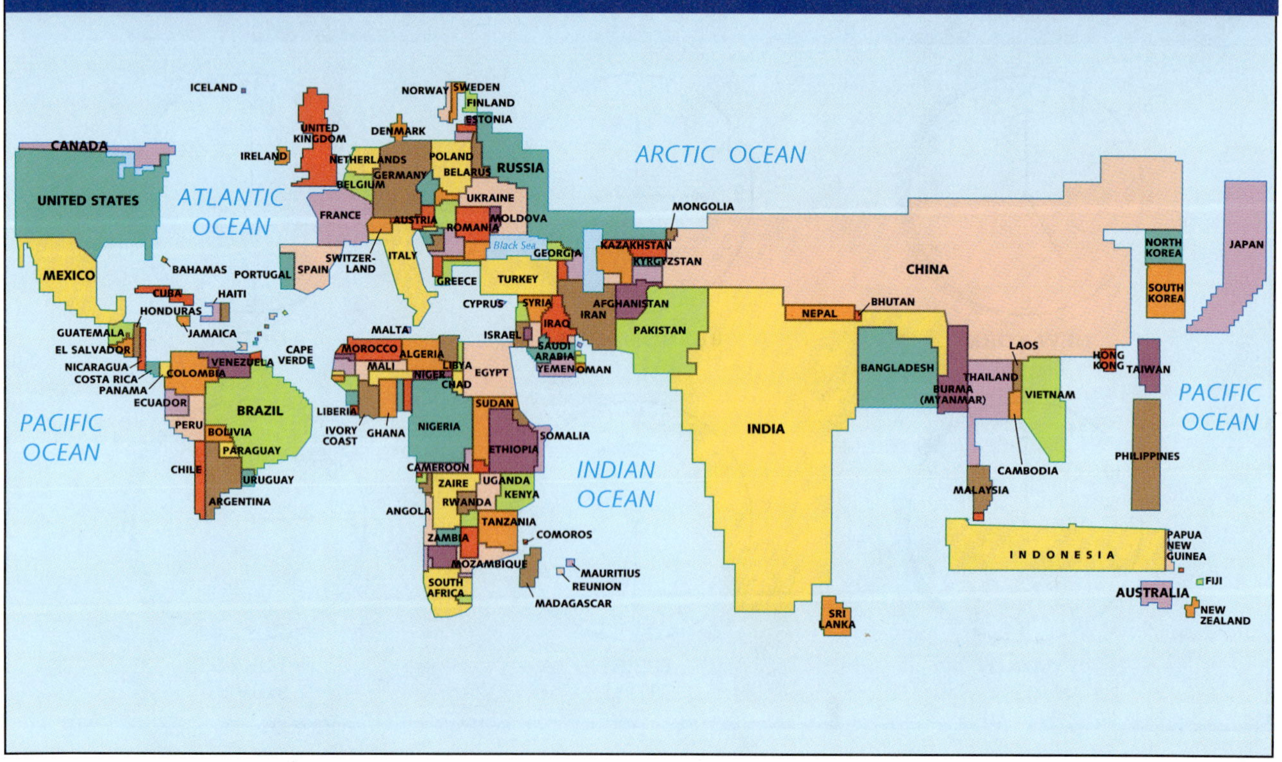

CARTOGRAM: GROSS DOMESTIC PRODUCT

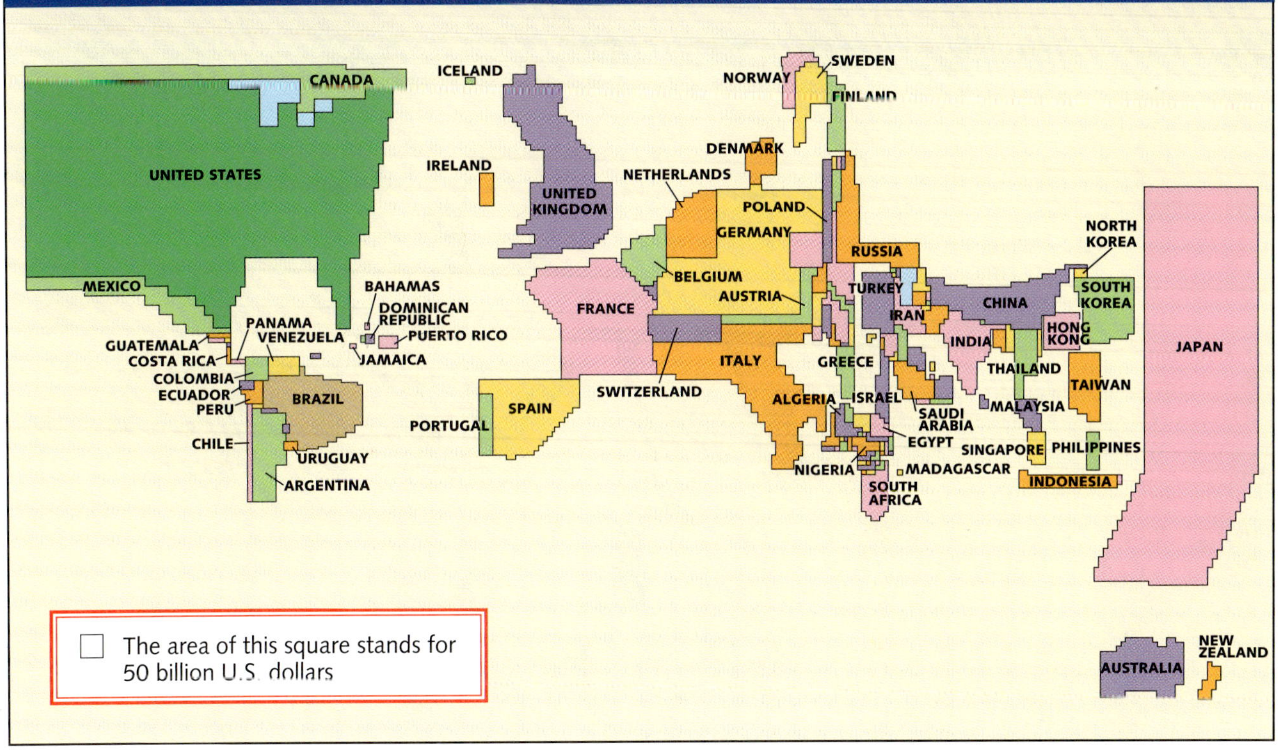

GDP FOR SELECTED COUNTRIES

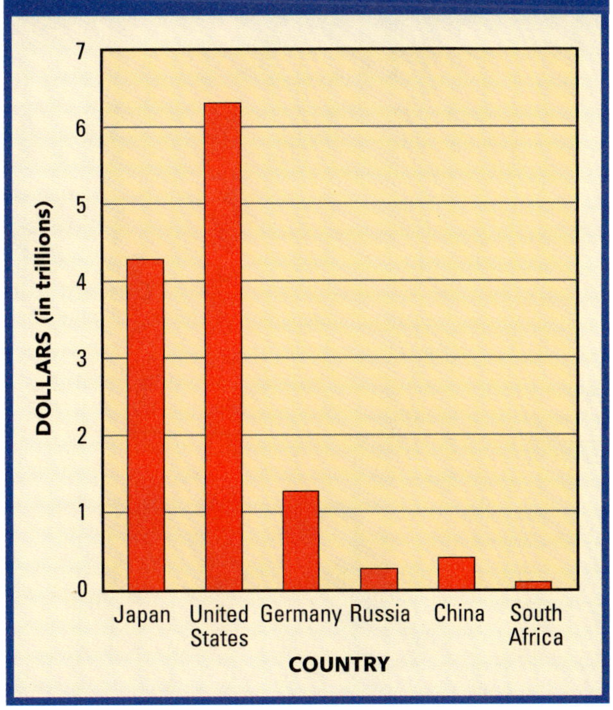

THE UNITED STATES

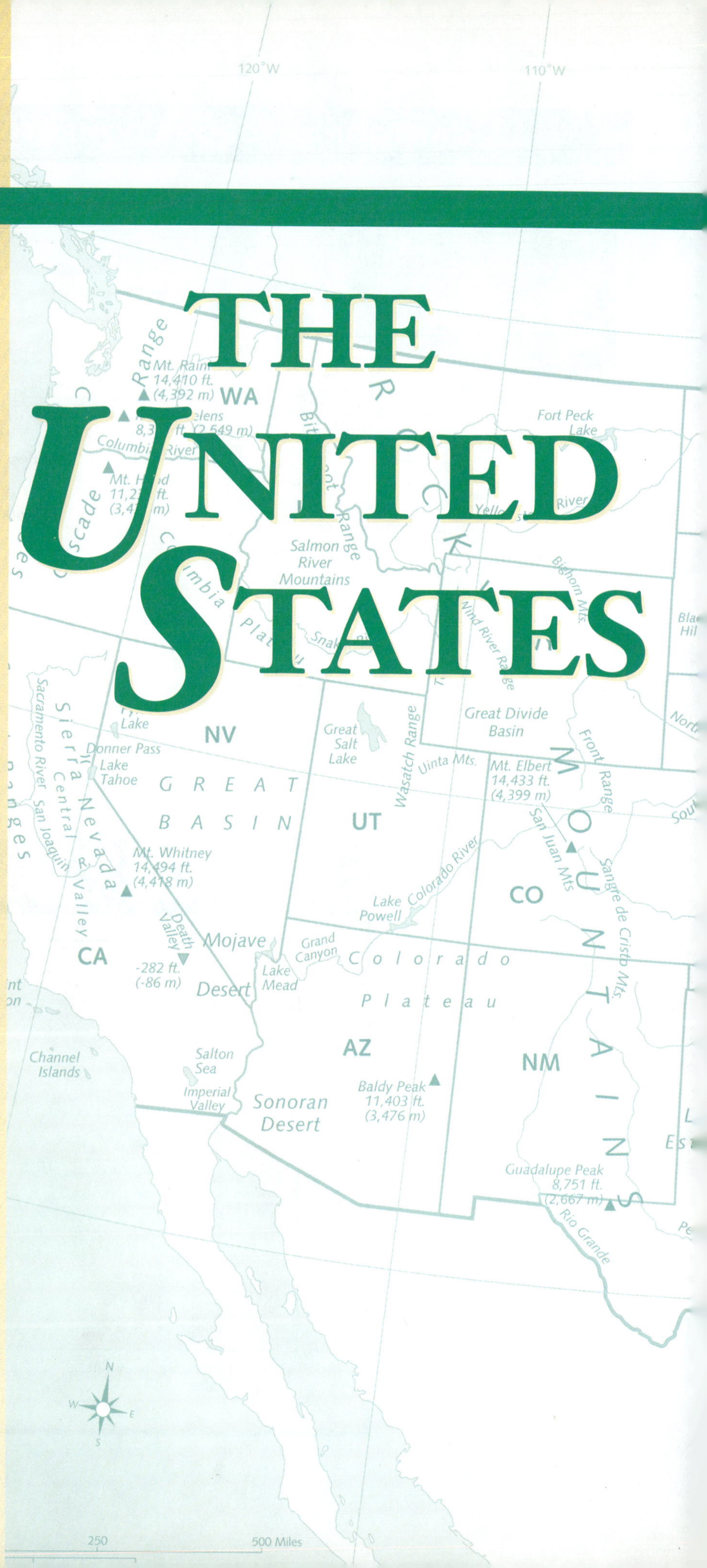

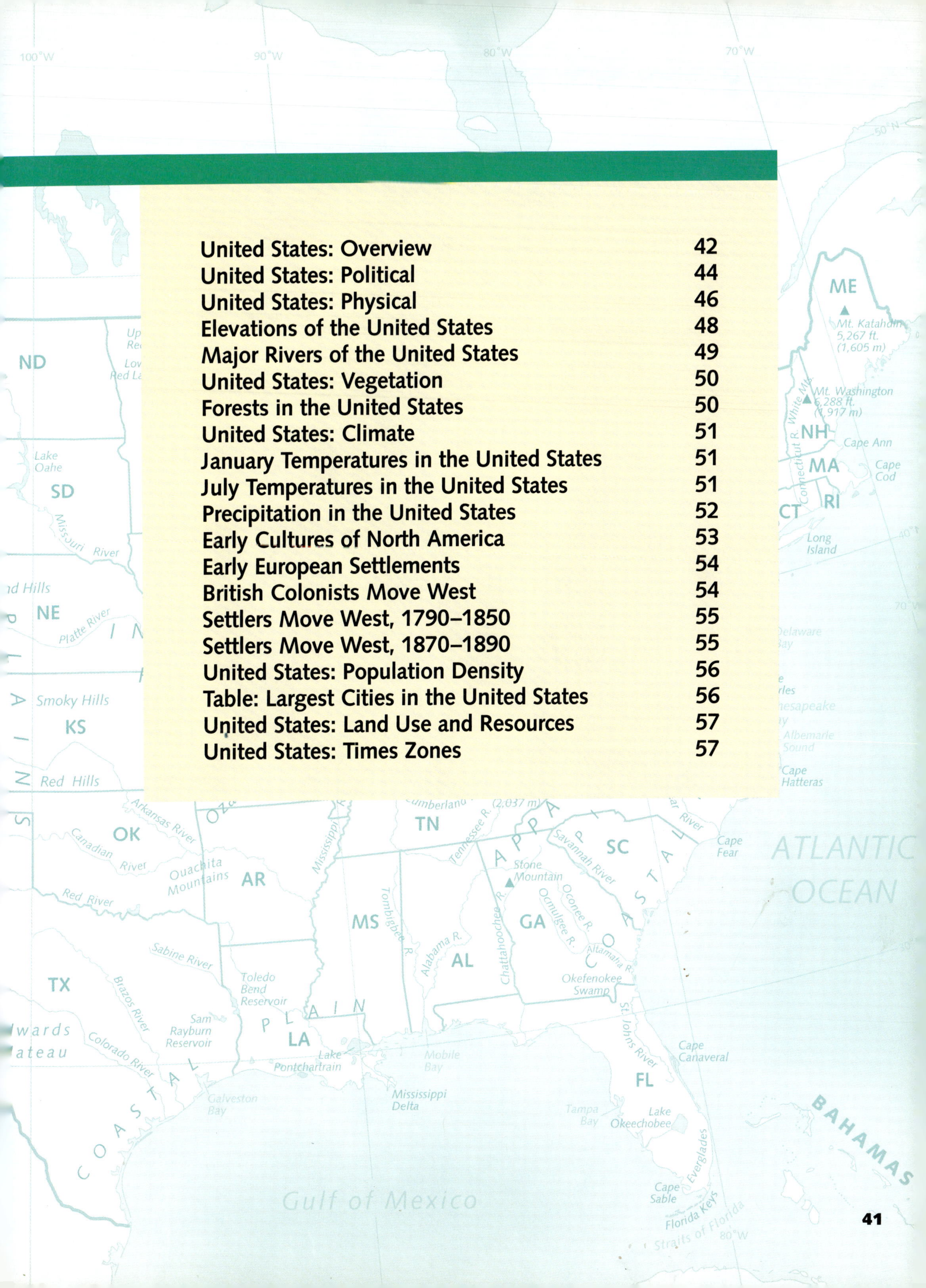
100°W
90°W
80°W
70°W
50°N
40°N
ND
SD
NE
KS
OK
TX
AR
LA
MS
AL
TN
GA
SC
FL
ME
NH
MA
RI
CT
Lake Oahe
Missouri River
Platte River
Smoky Hills
Red Hills
Arkansas River
Canadian River
Red River
Ouachita Mountains
Sabine River
Brazos River
Colorado River
Toledo Bend Reservoir
Sam Rayburn Reservoir
Galveston Bay
Lake Pontchartrain
Mobile Bay
Mississippi Delta
Gulf of Mexico
Tombigbee R.
Alabama R.
Chattahoochee R.
Tennessee R.
Stone Mountain
Savannah River
Oconee R.
Ocmulgee R.
Altamaha R.
Okefenokee Swamp
St. Johns River
Cape Canaveral
Tampa Bay
Lake Okeechobee
Everglades
Cape Sable
Florida Keys
Straits of Florida
BAHAMAS
ATLANTIC OCEAN
Cape Fear
Cape Hatteras
Albemarle Sound
Long Island
Cape Ann
Cape Cod
Connecticut R.
White Mts.
Mt. Katahdin 5,267 ft. (1,605 m)
Mt. Washington 6,288 ft. (1,917 m)

UNITED STATES: OVERVIEW

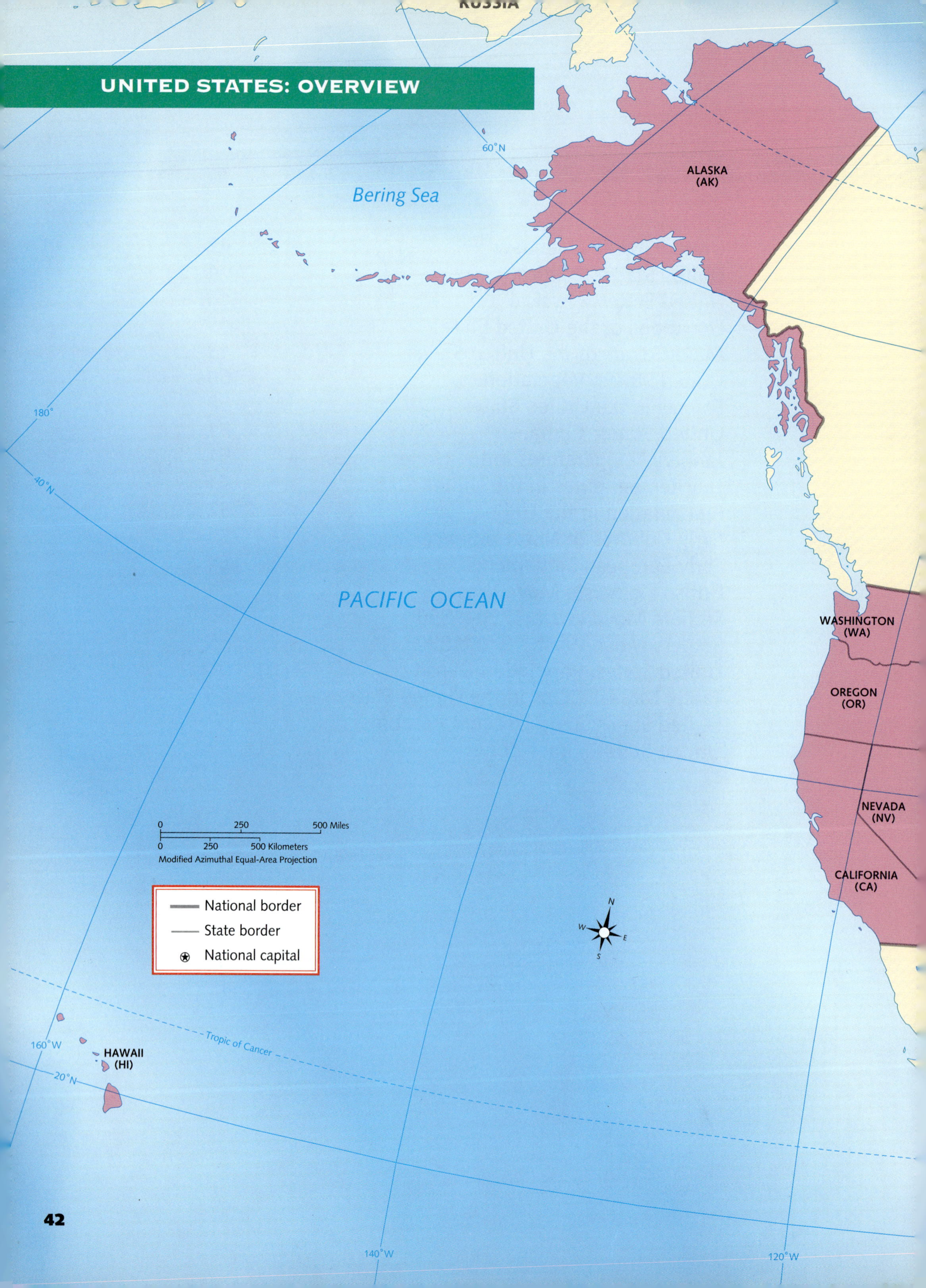

ICELAND
Arctic Circle
Greenland
60°N
40°W
Hudson Bay
CANADA
MONTANA (MT)
NORTH DAKOTA (ND)
MINNESOTA (MN)
Lake Superior
MICHIGAN
Lake Huron
VERMONT (VT)
MAINE (ME)
WISCONSIN (WI)
Lake Michigan
Lake Ontario
NEW YORK (NY)
NEW HAMPSHIRE (NH)
60°W
IDAHO (ID)
SOUTH DAKOTA (SD)
WYOMING (WY)
(MI)
MASSACHUSETTS (MA)
RHODE ISLAND (RI)
40°N
NEBRASKA (NE)
IOWA (IA)
Lake Erie
PENNSYLVANIA (PA)
NEW JERSEY (NJ)
CONNECTICUT (CT)
ILLINOIS (IL)
INDIANA (IN)
OHIO (OH)
Washington, D.C.
DELAWARE (DE)
UTAH (UT)
COLORADO (CO)
KANSAS (KS)
MISSOURI (MO)
WEST VIRGINIA (WV)
VIRGINIA (VA)
MARYLAND (MD)
KENTUCKY (KY)
NORTH CAROLINA (NC)
TENNESSEE (TN)
OKLAHOMA (OK)
ARIZONA (AZ)
NEW MEXICO (NM)
ARKANSAS (AR)
SOUTH CAROLINA (SC)
MISSISSIPPI (MS)
GEORGIA (GA)
ALABAMA (AL)
ATLANTIC OCEAN
TEXAS (TX)
LOUISIANA (LA)
FLORIDA (FL)
Gulf of Mexico
MEXICO
CUBA
DOMINICAN REPUBLIC
20°N
PUERTO RICO
HAITI
100°W
80°W

UNITED STATES: POLITICAL

CANADA
Lake Superior
Lake Michigan
Lake Huron
Lake Ontario
Lake Erie
North Dakota (ND)
Bismarck
Minnesota (MN)
St. Paul
South Dakota (SD)
Pierre
Wisconsin (WI)
Madison
Michigan
(MI)
Lansing
Iowa (IA)
Des Moines
Nebraska (NE)
Lincoln
Illinois (IL)
Springfield
Indiana (IN)
Indianapolis
Ohio (OH)
Columbus
Pennsylvania (PA)
Harrisburg
New York (NY)
Albany
Vermont (VT)
Montpelier
Maine (ME)
Augusta
New Hampshire (NH)
Concord
Massachusetts (MA)
Boston
Rhode Island (RI)
Providence
Connecticut (CT)
Hartford
New Jersey (NJ)
Trenton
Delaware (DE)
Dover
Maryland (MD)
Annapolis
Washington, D.C.
West Virginia (WV)
Charleston
Virginia (VA)
Richmond
Kansas (KS)
Topeka
Missouri (MO)
Jefferson City
Kentucky (KY)
Frankfort
North Carolina (NC)
Raleigh
Tennessee (TN)
Nashville
Oklahoma (OK)
Oklahoma City
Arkansas (AR)
Little Rock
South Carolina (SC)
Columbia
Atlanta
Georgia (GA)
Mississippi (MS)
Jackson
Alabama (AL)
Montgomery
Texas (TX)
Austin
Louisiana (LA)
Baton Rouge
Tallahassee
Florida (FL)
ATLANTIC OCEAN
BAHAMAS
Gulf of Mexico
CUBA

UNITED STATES: PHYSICAL

100°W
90°W
80°W
70°W
50°N
40°N
30°N
70°W
80°W
100°W
90°W
CANADA
ND
SD
NE
KS
OK
TX
MN
IA
MO
AR
LA
WI
IL
MS
MI
IN
KY
TN
AL
OH
WV
GA
FL
PA
VA
NC
SC
NY
VT
NH
ME
MA
CT
RI
NJ
MD
DE
GREAT PLAINS
INTERIOR PLAINS
CENTRAL PLAINS
COASTAL PLAIN
PIEDMONT
APPALACHIAN MOUNTAINS
Lake of the Woods
Upper Red Lake
Lower Red Lake
Leech Lake
Mesabi Range
Mille Lacs Lake
Isle Royale
Lake Superior
Keweenaw Peninsula
Upper Peninsula
Lake Michigan
Lower Peninsula
Lake Huron
Lake St. Clair
Lake Erie
Lake Ontario
Niagara Falls
Finger Lakes
Lake Winnebago
Wisconsin River
Mississippi River
Lake Oahe
Missouri River
Sand Hills
North Platte R.
Platte River
South Platte R.
Smoky Hills
Red Hills
Llano Estacado
Edwards Plateau
Pecos River
Arkansas River
Canadian River
Red River
Ouachita Mountains
Ozark Plateau
Harry S. Truman Reservoir
Lake of the Ozarks
Missouri River
Illinois River
Wabash River
Ohio River
Cumberland Gap
Lake Barkley
Cumberland R.
Tennessee R.
Mt. Mitchell 6,684 ft. (2,037 m)
Stone Mountain
Savannah River
Oconee R.
Ocmulgee R.
Altamaha R.
Okefenokee Swamp
Chattahoochee R.
Alabama R.
Tombigbee R.
Mississippi River
Sabine River
Toledo Bend Reservoir
Sam Rayburn Reservoir
Brazos River
Colorado River
Galveston Bay
Lake Pontchartrain
Mississippi Delta
Mobile Bay
Gulf of Mexico
Tampa Bay
Lake Okeechobee
St. Johns River
Cape Canaveral
Everglades
Cape Sable
Florida Keys
Straits of Florida
CUBA
BAHAMAS
ATLANTIC OCEAN
Cape Fear
Cape Fear River
Cape Hatteras
Roanoke R.
Albemarle Sound
James R.
Chesapeake Bay
Cape Charles
Potomac R.
Allegheny Mts.
Delaware Bay
Long Island
Hudson R.
Adirondack Mountains
Lake Champlain
St. Lawrence River
Green Mts.
Connecticut R.
White Mts.
Mt. Washington 6,288 ft. (1,917 m)
Mt. Katahdin 5,267 ft. (1,605 m)
Cape Ann
Cape Cod
Black Hills

ELEVATIONS OF THE UNITED STATES

MAJOR RIVERS OF THE UNITED STATES

UNITED STATES: VEGETATION
Forest
Grassland
Desert
Tundra
RUSSIA
ARCTIC OCEAN
CANADA
PACIFIC OCEAN
0 200 400 Miles
0 400 Kilometers
CANADA
Lake Superior
Lake Michigan
Lake Huron
Lake Ontario
Lake Erie
130°W
40°N
70°W
PACIFIC OCEAN
ATLANTIC OCEAN
30°N
120°W
MEXICO
0 200 400 Miles
0 200 400 Kilometers
Albers Equal-Area Projection
0 100 Miles
0 100 Kilometers
110°W
90°W
80°W
Gulf of Mexico
N
E
W
S

FORESTS IN THE UNITED STATES
RUSSIA
ALASKA
PACIFIC OCEAN
0 200 400 Miles
0 200 400 Kilometers
Albers Equal-Area Projection
Forest
CANADA
ROCKY MOUNTAINS
APPALACHIAN MOUNTAINS
ATLANTIC OCEAN
PACIFIC OCEAN
HAWAII
MEXICO
Gulf of Mexico
N
E
W
S

UNITED STATES: CLIMATE

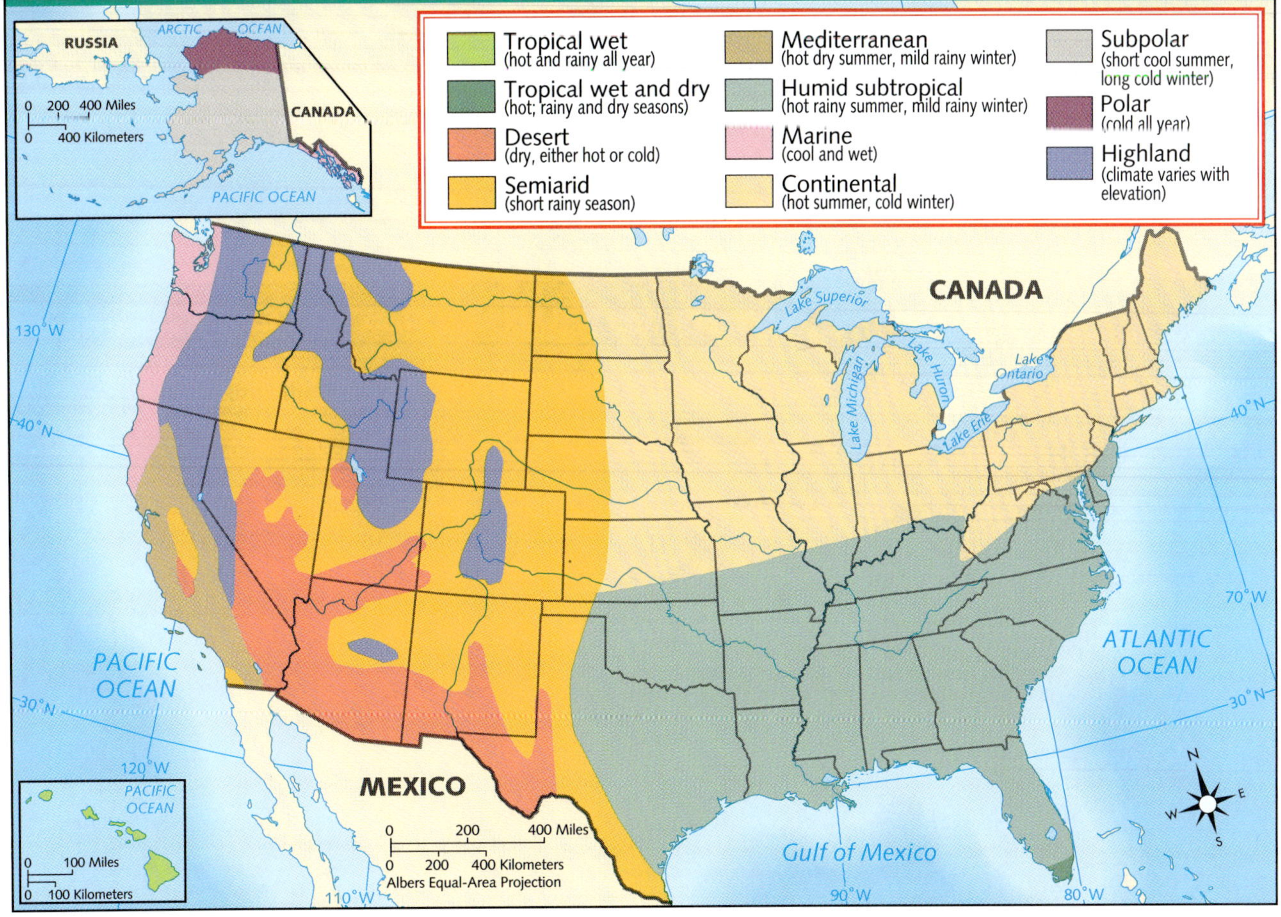

JANUARY TEMPERATURES IN THE UNITED STATES

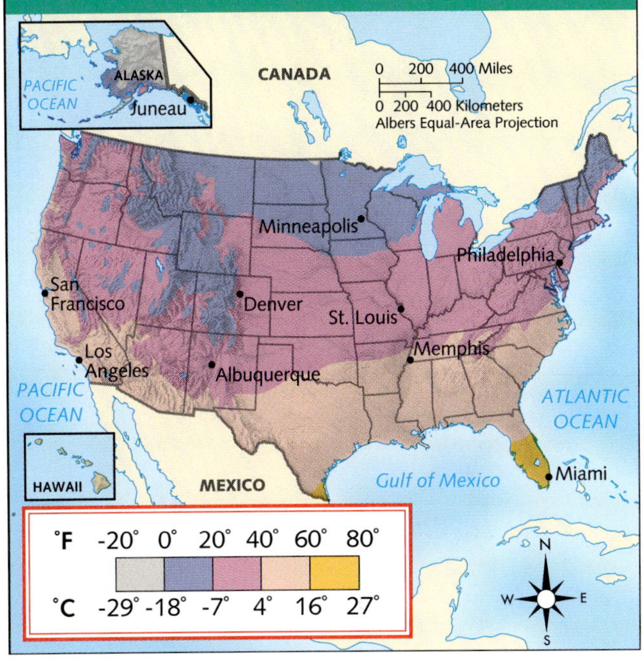

JULY TEMPERATURES IN THE UNITED STATES

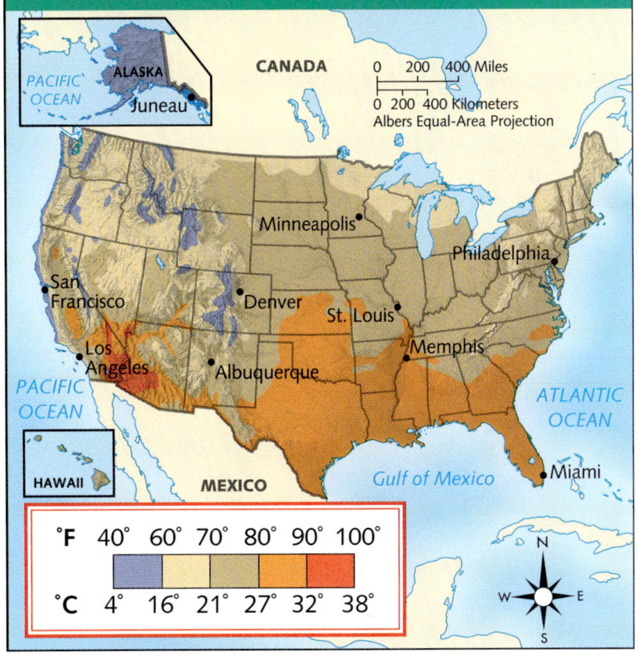

PRECIPITATION IN THE UNITED STATES

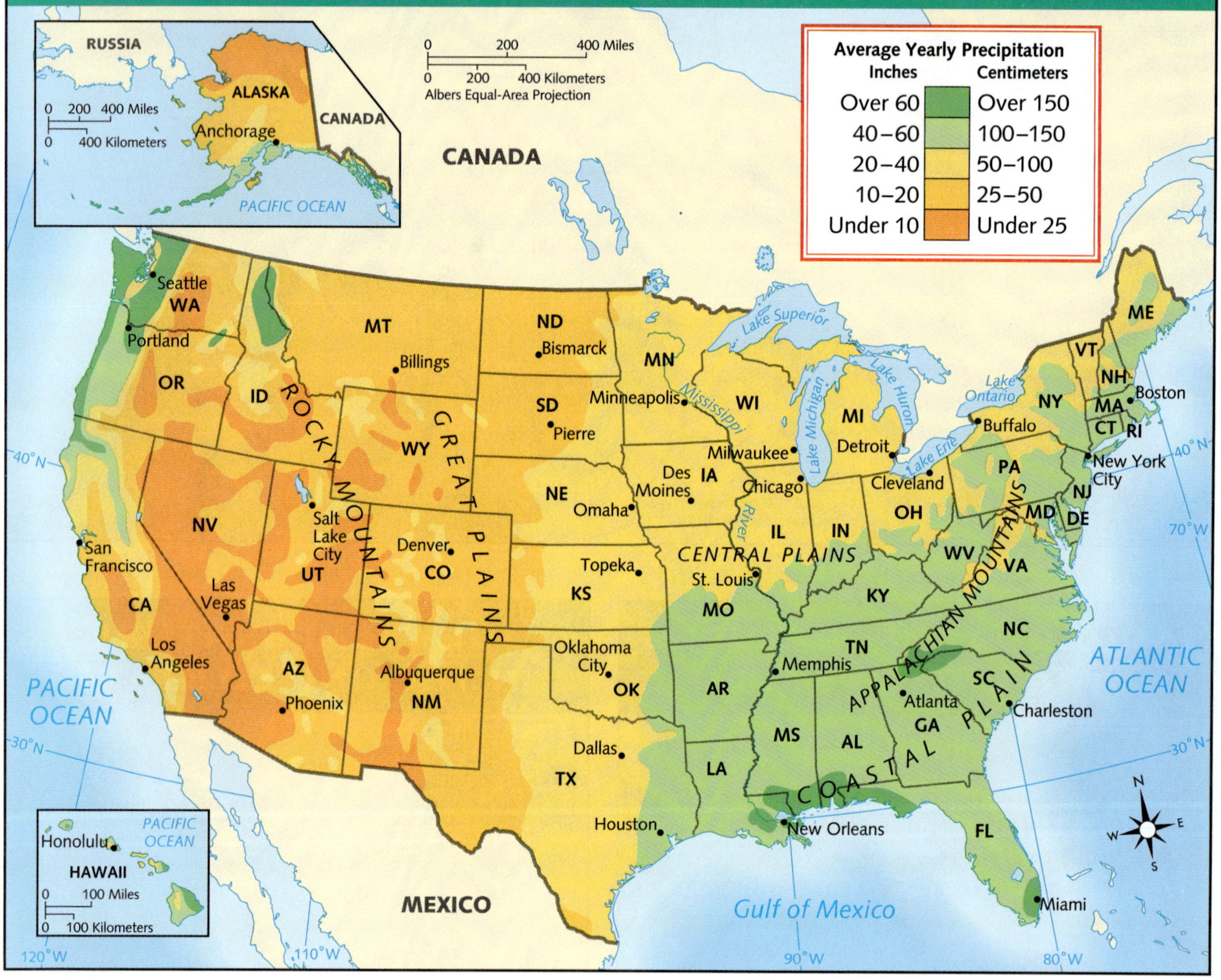

EARLY CULTURES OF NORTH AMERICA

EARLY EUROPEAN SETTLEMENTS

BRITISH COLONISTS MOVE WEST

SETTLERS MOVE WEST, 1790–1850

SETTLERS MOVE WEST, 1870–1890

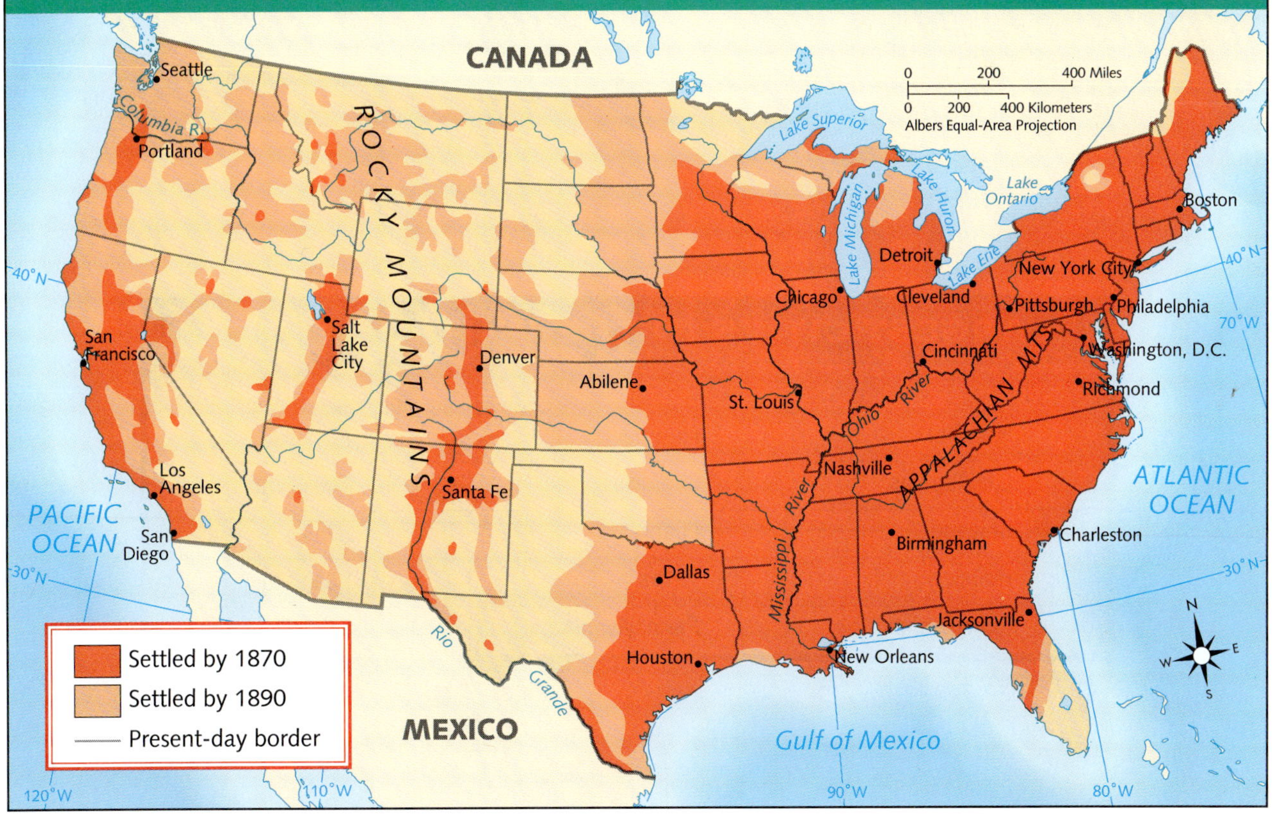

UNITED STATES: POPULATION DENSITY

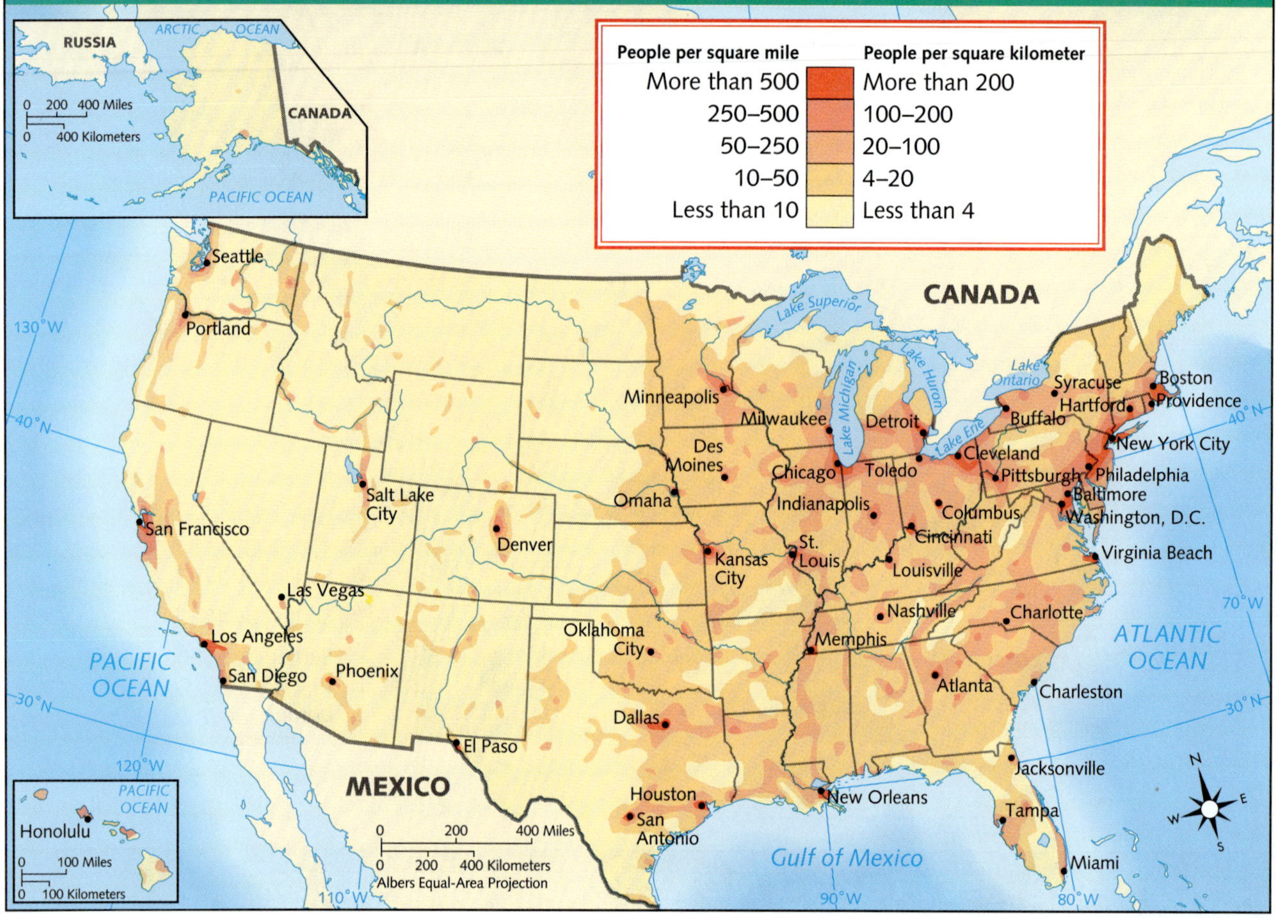

LARGEST CITIES IN THE UNITED STATES

CITY	STATE	POPULATION*
New York	New York	7,311,966
Los Angeles	California	3,489,779
Chicago	Illinois	2,768,483
Houston	Texas	1,690,180
Philadelphia	Pennsylvania	1,552,572

*The most recent figures available

UNITED STATES: LAND USE AND RESOURCES

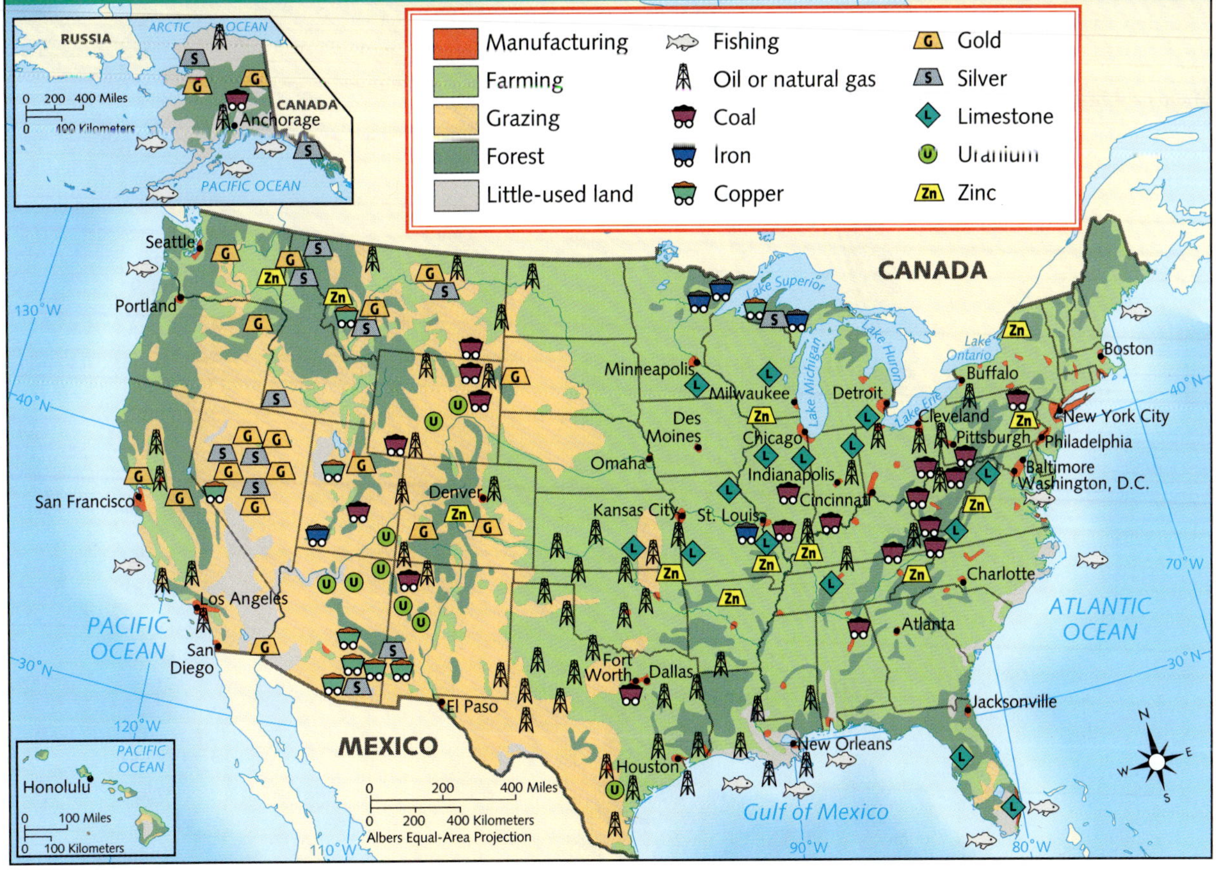

UNITED STATES TIME ZONES

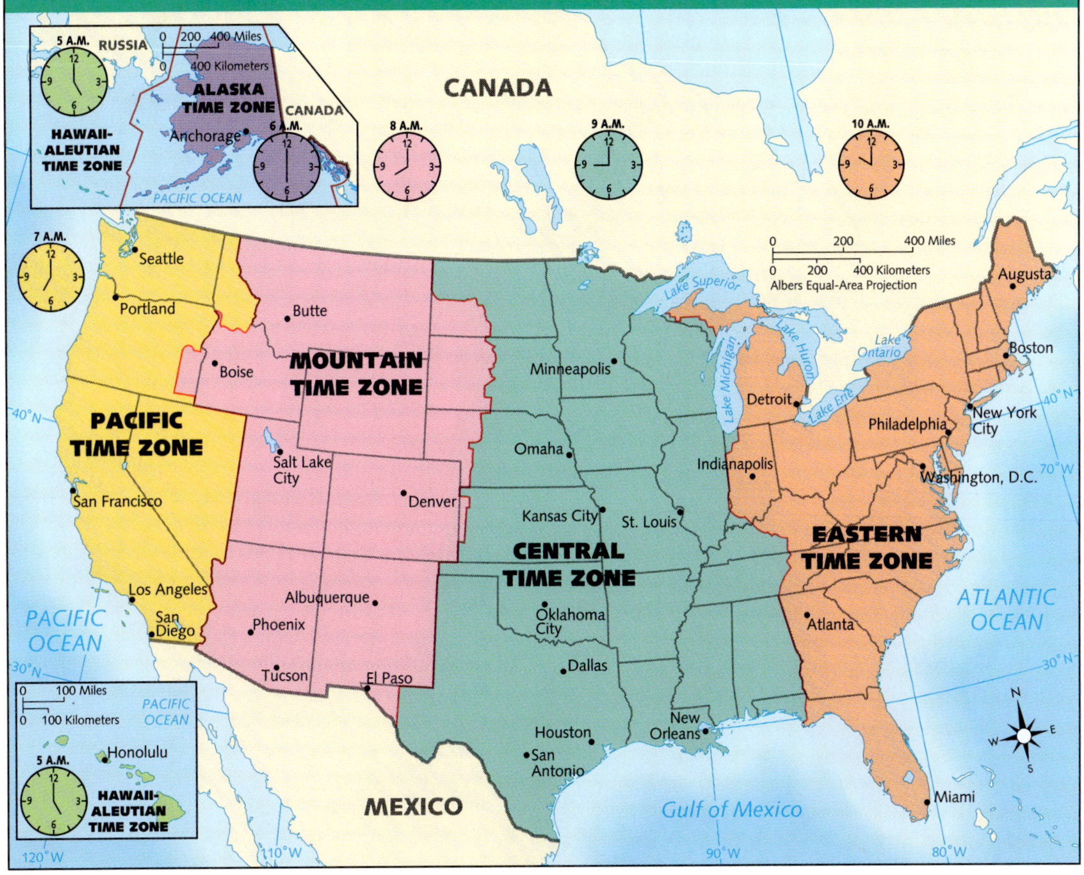

UNITED STATES REGIONS

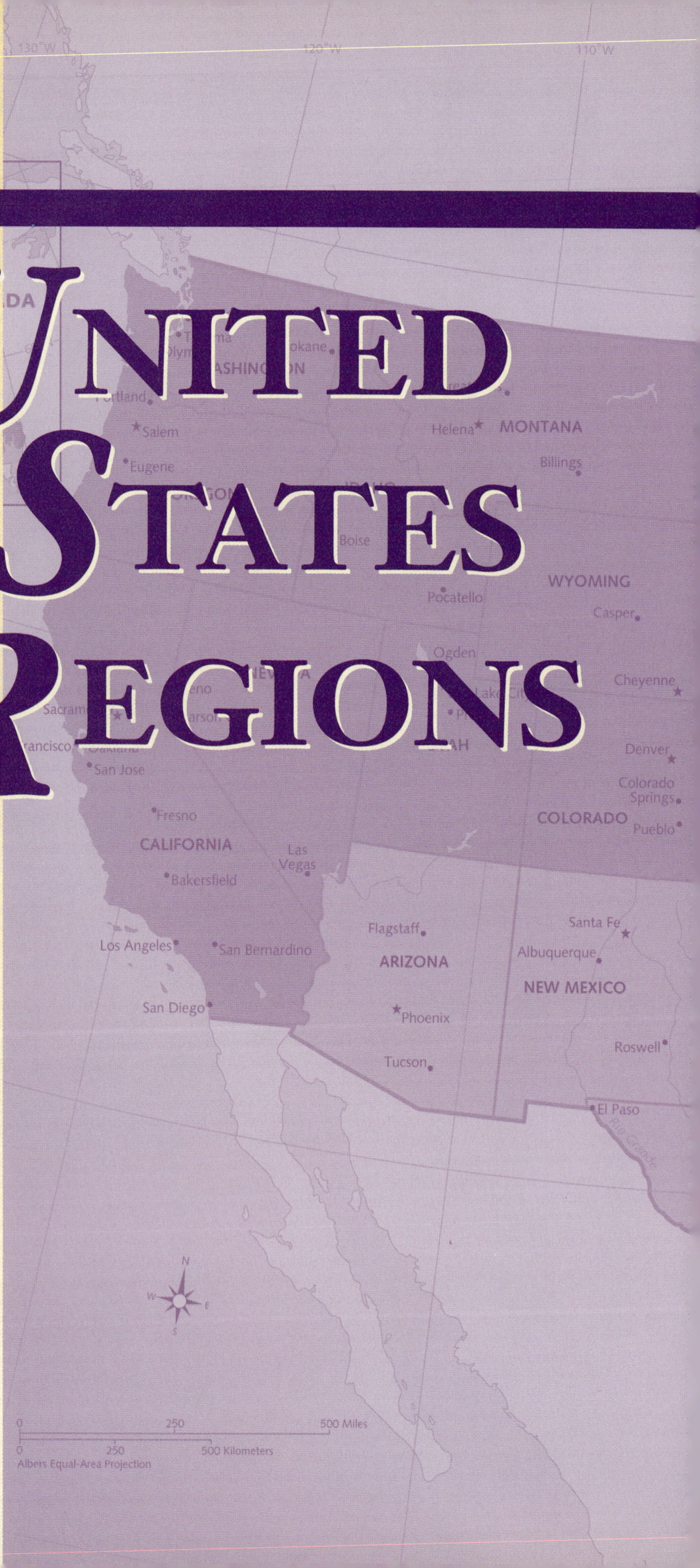

UNITED STATES: REGIONS

CANADA
ATLANTIC OCEAN
Gulf of Mexico
BAHAMAS
CUBA
100°W
90°W
80°W
70°W
50°N
40°N
30°N
70°W
80°W
Lake Superior
Lake Michigan
Lake Huron
Lake Erie
Lake Ontario
St. Lawrence River
Mississippi River
Missouri River
Platte River
Arkansas River
Red River
Ohio River
Tennessee River
Lake Okeechobee
NORTH DAKOTA
Grand Forks
Fargo
Bismarck
SOUTH DAKOTA
Rapid City
Pierre
Sioux Falls
MINNESOTA
Duluth
St. Paul
Minneapolis
WISCONSIN
Green Bay
Madison
Milwaukee
MICHIGAN
Sault Sainte Marie
Grand Rapids
Lansing
Flint
Detroit
NEBRASKA
Omaha
Lincoln
IOWA
Sioux City
Cedar Rapids
Davenport
Des Moines
ILLINOIS
Rockford
Chicago
Peoria
Decatur
Springfield
INDIANA
Gary
South Bend
Indianapolis
Evansville
OHIO
Toledo
Cleveland
Akron
Columbus
Dayton
Cincinnati
KANSAS
Topeka
Wichita
MISSOURI
Kansas City
Jefferson City
St. Louis
Springfield
KENTUCKY
Louisville
Frankfort
Lexington
WEST VIRGINIA
Wheeling
Charleston
PENNSYLVANIA
Pittsburgh
Harrisburg
Philadelphia
NEW YORK
Buffalo
Rochester
Syracuse
Albany
New York City
VERMONT
Burlington
Montpelier
NEW HAMPSHIRE
Manchester
Concord
MAINE
Augusta
Portland
MASSACHUSETTS
Worcester
Boston
RHODE ISLAND
Providence
CONNECTICUT
Hartford
Bridgeport
NEW JERSEY
Newark
Trenton
DELAWARE
Wilmington
Dover
MARYLAND
Baltimore
Annapolis
Washington, D.C.
VIRGINIA
Richmond
Roanoke
Newport News
Norfolk
NORTH CAROLINA
Greensboro
Winston-Salem
Raleigh
Charlotte
SOUTH CAROLINA
Columbia
Charleston
TENNESSEE
Knoxville
Nashville
Chattanooga
Memphis
OKLAHOMA
Tulsa
Oklahoma City
ARKANSAS
Fort Smith
Little Rock
MISSISSIPPI
Meridian
Jackson
Biloxi
ALABAMA
Huntsville
Birmingham
Montgomery
Mobile
GEORGIA
Atlanta
Macon
Columbus
Savannah
FLORIDA
Jacksonville
Tallahassee
Orlando
Tampa
St. Petersburg
West Palm Beach
Miami
LOUISIANA
Shreveport
Baton Rouge
New Orleans
TEXAS
Amarillo
Lubbock
Fort Worth
Dallas
Abilene
Odessa
Austin
Beaumont
Houston
San Antonio
Laredo
Corpus Christi

THE NORTHEAST

REGION

Did You Know?

There are 11 states in the Northeast. Of those states, 6 are known together as the New England states. The other 5 states are known as the Middle Atlantic states. The nation's capital, Washington, D.C., is also a part of the Northeast.

STATE	CAPITAL	NICKNAME	POPULATION*
THE NEW ENGLAND STATES			
Connecticut (CT)	Hartford	Constitution State	3,268,000
Maine (ME)	Augusta	Pine Tree State	1,236,000
Massachusetts (MA)	Boston	Bay State	5,959,000
New Hampshire (NH)	Concord	Granite State	1,144,000
Rhode Island (RI)	Providence	Ocean State	998,000
Vermont (VT)	Montpelier	Green Mountain State	584,000
THE MIDDLE ATLANTIC STATES			
Delaware (DE)	Dover	First State	736,000
Maryland (MD)	Annapolis	Old Line State	5,180,000
New Jersey (NJ)	Trenton	Garden State	8,015,000
New York (NY)	Albany	Empire State	18,198,000
Pennsylvania (PA)	Harrisburg	Keystone State	12,210,000

*The most recent figures available

TEN LARGEST CITIES

1. New York, New York
2. Philadelphia, Pennsylvania
3. Baltimore, Maryland
4. Washington, D.C.,
5. Boston, Massachusetts
6. Pittsburgh, Pennsylvania
7. Buffalo, New York
8. Newark, New Jersey
9. Rochester, New York
10. Jersey City, New Jersey

LEADING PRODUCTS AND RESOURCES

Farming: Apples, beef cattle, blueberries, cranberries, dairy cows, potatoes, poultry
Fishing: Clams, crabs, fish, lobsters, scallops
Manufacturing: Chemicals, clothing, dairy products, electrical equipment, lumber, maple syrup, medicines, paper products, plastics, printed materials, processed foods
Mining: Coal, gravel, iron, natural gas, oil, sand, stone, zinc

The Verrazano-Narrows Bridge, in New York, has the longest span of any bridge in the United States—4,260 feet (1,298 m).

Ice was an important "crop" in the Northeast. In the days before electric refrigerators, ice was used to cool food. It was cut from frozen rivers and lakes and shipped to places all over the United States. In 1890, 3 million tons were cut in the state of Maine alone.

New York City has more people than any other city in the United States. More than 7 million people live there.

NEW ENGLAND ELEVATIONS
Feet
Meters
Above 1,640
655
0
Above 500
200
0
Below sea level
CANADA
St. Lawrence River
St. John River
Caribou
MAINE
Bangor
VERMONT
Burlington
Lake Champlain
Green Mountains
Connecticut River
White Mountains
Mt. Washington 6,288 ft. (1,917 m)
Portland
NY
NEW HAMPSHIRE
Manchester
Boston Harbor
ATLANTIC OCEAN
Boston
MASSACHUSETTS
Massachusetts Bay
Hudson River
Hartford
CONNECTICUT
Providence
RHODE ISLAND
Cape Cod
COASTAL PLAIN
Long Island Sound
0 50 100 Miles
0 50 100 Kilometers
Albers Equal-Area Projection
N
W
E
S

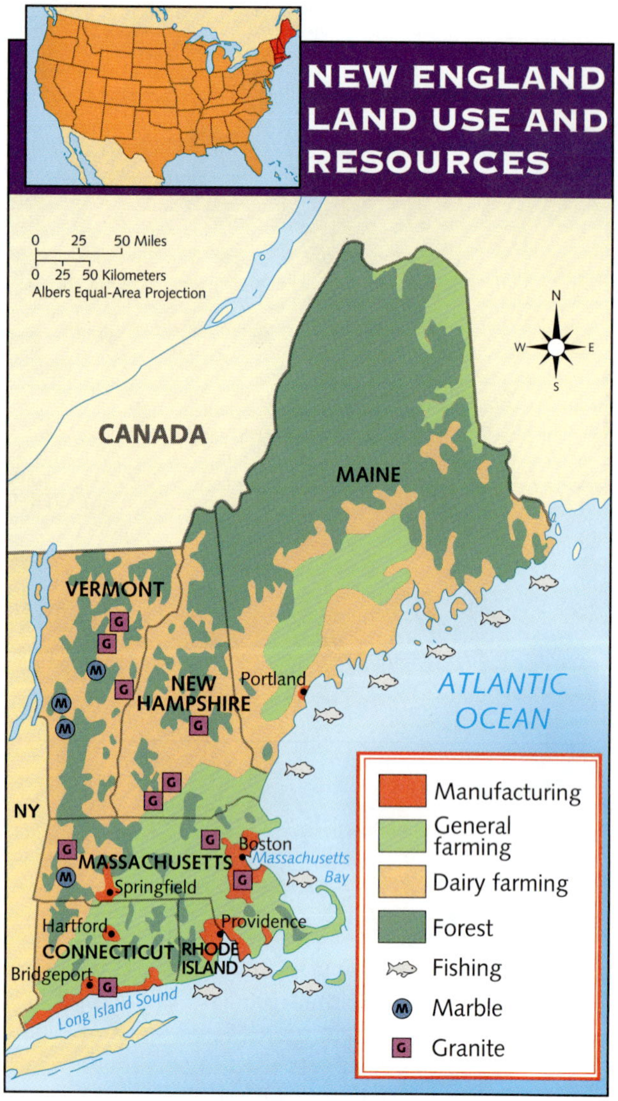
NEW ENGLAND LAND USE AND RESOURCES
0 25 50 Miles
0 25 50 Kilometers
Albers Equal-Area Projection
N
W
E
S
CANADA
MAINE
VERMONT
NEW HAMPSHIRE
Portland
ATLANTIC OCEAN
NY
MASSACHUSETTS
Boston
Massachusetts Bay
Springfield
Hartford
Providence
CONNECTICUT
RHODE ISLAND
Bridgeport
Long Island Sound
Manufacturing
General farming
Dairy farming
Forest
Fishing
Marble
Granite

MIDDLE ATLANTIC ELEVATIONS

MIDDLE ATLANTIC LAND USE AND RESOURCES

THE SOUTHEAST REGION

Did You Know?

There are 12 states in the Southeast. Virginia, North Carolina, South Carolina, and Georgia are 4 of the 13 original states. Georgia is the largest state in the Southeast. Florida, however, has the most people.

THE SOUTHEAST STATES

STATE	CAPITAL	NICKNAME	POPULATION*
Alabama (AL)	Montgomery	Heart of Dixie	4,361,000
Arkansas (AR)	Little Rock	Land of Opportunity	2,513,000
Florida (FL)	Tallahassee	Sunshine State	14,663,000
Georgia (GA)	Atlanta	Empire State of the South	7,324,000
Kentucky (KY)	Frankfort	Bluegrass State	3,911,000
Louisiana (LA)	Baton Rouge	Pelican State	4,404,000
Mississippi (MS)	Jackson	Magnolia State	2,700,000
North Carolina (NC)	Raleigh	Tar Heel State	7,347,000
South Carolina (SC)	Columbia	Palmetto State	3,814,000
Tennessee (TN)	Nashville	Volunteer State	5,359,000
Virginia (VA)	Richmond	Old Dominion	6,814,000
West Virginia (WV)	Charleston	Mountain State	1,832,000

*The most recent figures available.

TEN LARGEST CITIES

1. Jacksonville, Florida
2. Memphis, Tennessee
3. Nashville-Davidson, Tennessee
4. New Orleans, Louisiana
5. Virginia Beach, Virginia
6. Charlotte, North Carolina
7. Atlanta, Georgia
8. Miami, Florida
9. Tampa, Florida
10. Louisville, Kentucky

LEADING PRODUCTS AND RESOURCES

Farming: Beef cattle, citrus fruits, cotton, dairy cows, hogs, horses, peanuts, poultry, rice, soybeans, sugarcane, tobacco, vegetables
Fishing: Clams, crabs, fish, lobsters, scallops, shrimp
Manufacturing: Chemicals, dairy products, electrical equipment, furniture, glass, lumber, paper products, plastics, processed foods, textiles
Mining: Coal, iron, limestone, natural gas, oil, phosphates, zinc

Most of the glass marbles manufactured in the United States are made in West Virginia.

The largest sculpture in the world is carved on the face of Stone Mountain, in Georgia. Stone Mountain is the largest mass of granite in North America.

THE SOUTHEAST

Mammoth Cave, in Kentucky, is part of the world's largest known cave system.

St. Augustine, Florida, is the oldest permanent settlement built by Europeans in what is today the United States. It was settled by the Spanish in 1565.

The manatee is an endangered sea mammal found near Florida's coasts.

MAJOR PORTS OF THE SOUTHEAST

PUERTO RICO AND THE VIRGIN ISLANDS

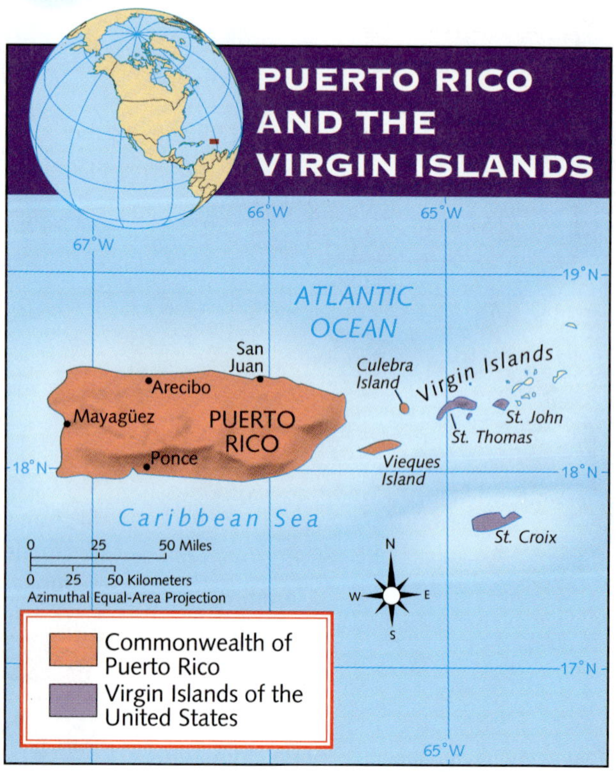

SOUTHEAST LAND USE AND RESOURCES

LEADING CHICKEN-PRODUCING STATES

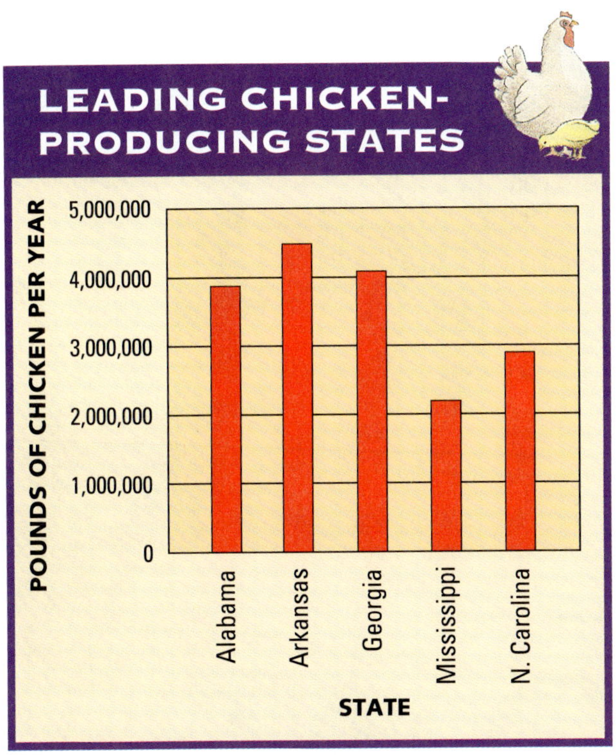

TENNESSEE VALLEY AUTHORITY

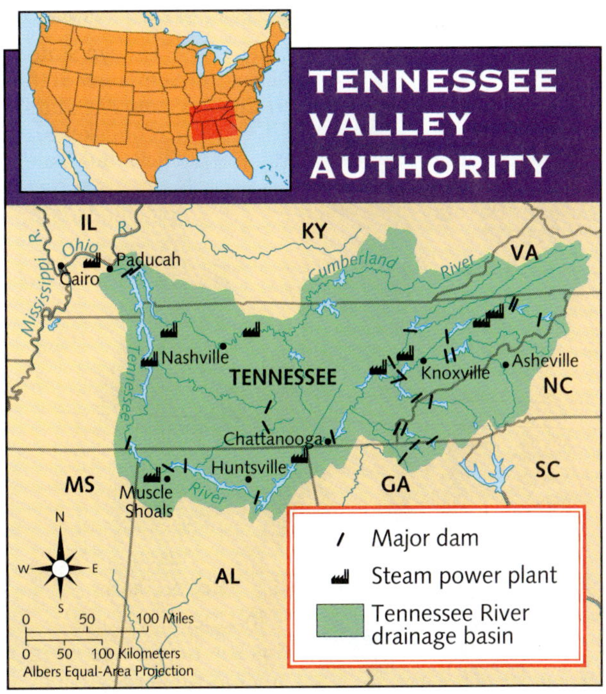

REGION

Did You Know?

Twelve states make up the Middle West. Sometimes those states are divided into two smaller regions—the Plains states and the Great Lakes states. All six Great Lakes states border a Great Lake.

STATE	CAPITAL	NICKNAME	POPULATION*
THE GREAT LAKES STATES			
Illinois (IL)	Springfield	Land of Lincoln	11,989,000
Indiana (IN)	Indianapolis	Hoosier State	5,920,000
Michigan (MI)	Lansing	Wolverine State	9,656,000
Minnesota (MN)	St. Paul	Gopher State	4,706,000
Ohio (OH)	Columbus	Buckeye State	11,318,000
Wisconsin (WI)	Madison	Badger State	5,256,000
THE PLAINS STATES			
Iowa (IA)	Des Moines	Hawkeye State	2,893,000
Kansas (KS)	Topeka	Sunflower State	2,652,000
Missouri (MO)	Jefferson City	Show Me State	5,347,000
Nebraska (NE)	Lincoln	Cornhusker State	1,670,000
North Dakota (ND)	Bismarck	Flickertail State	639,000
South Dakota (SD)	Pierre	Sunshine State	750,000

*The most recent figures available

TEN LARGEST CITIES

1. Chicago, Illinois
2. Detroit, Michigan
3. Indianapolis, Indiana
4. Columbus, Ohio
5. Milwaukee, Wisconsin
6. Cleveland, Ohio
7. Kansas City, Missouri
8. St. Louis, Missouri
9. Minneapolis, Minnesota
10. Cincinnati, Ohio

LEADING PRODUCTS AND RESOURCES

Farming:
Beef cattle, beets, corn, dairy cows, grain sorghum, hay, hogs, oats, poultry, sheep, soybeans, sunflower seeds, wheat
Manufacturing:
Automobiles, books, chemicals, dairy products, electrical equipment, machinery, metal products, packaged meats, paper products, processed foods
Mining:
Coal, copper, crushed stone, gold, iron, lead, limestone, natural gas, oil

The National Museum of Roller Skating is in Lincoln, Nebraska. It is the only museum in the world just for roller skating.

Ice-cream cones were first served at the 1904 Louisiana Purchase Exposition World's Fair in St. Louis, Missouri.

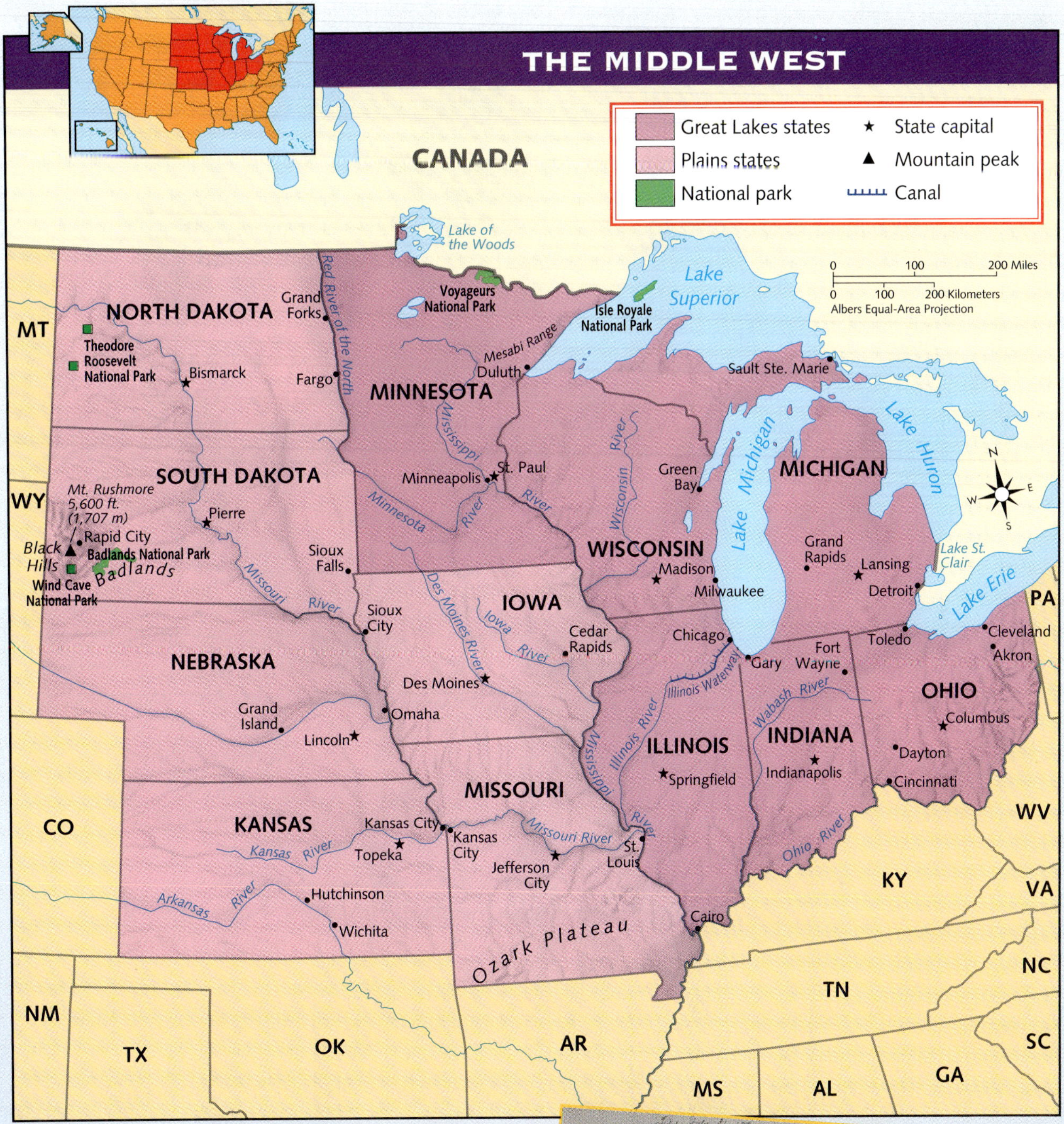

SIWINOWE

Kesibwi.

PALAKO WAHOSTOTA NAKOTE KESIBO.—WISELIBI. 1841.

J. LYKINS EDITOR. NOVEMBER. 1841. BAPTIST MISSION PRESS

The first newspaper in North America to be printed entirely in an Indian language was the *Siwinowe Kesibwi*, or "Shawnee Sun." It was first printed in Kansas in 1835.

In 1869 the Cincinnati Red Stockings, now the Cincinnati Reds, became the first professional baseball team.

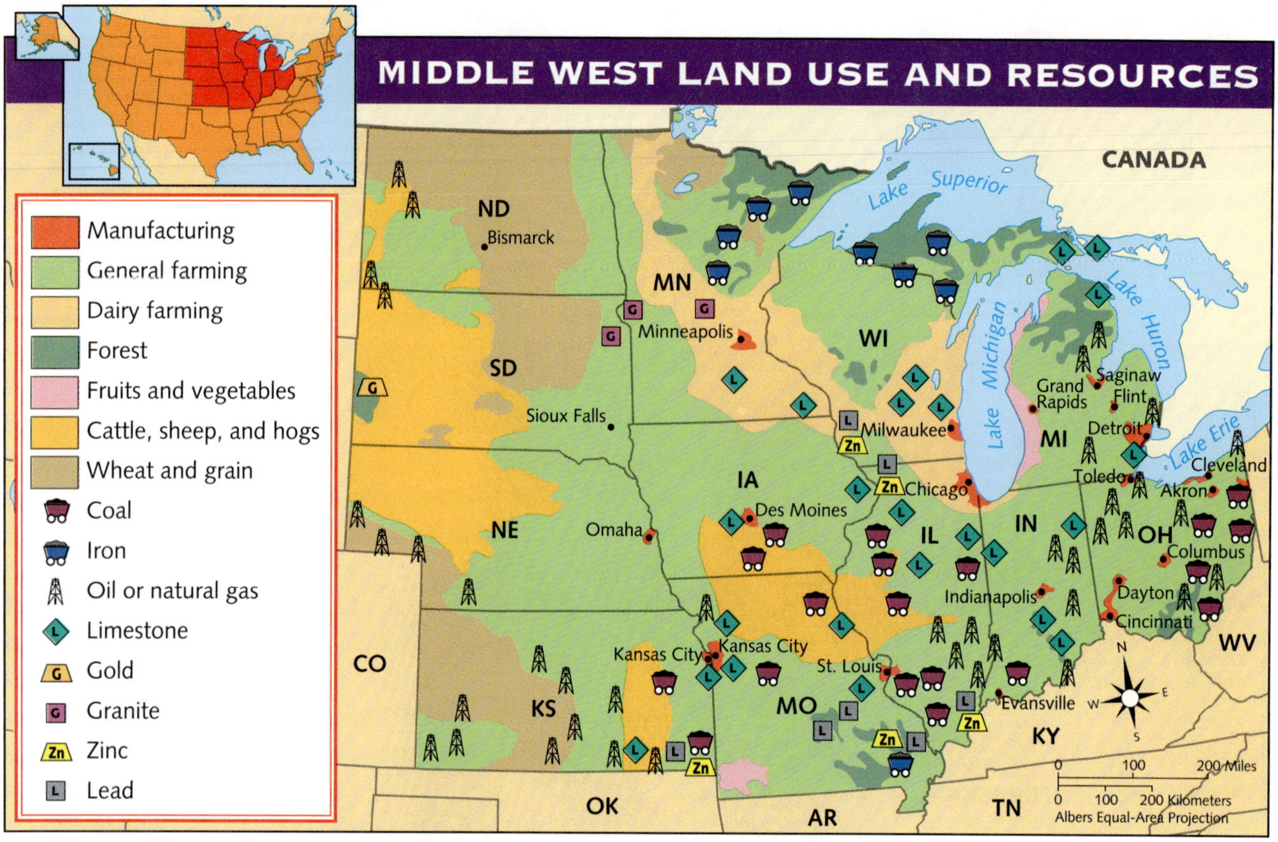
MIDDLE WEST LAND USE AND RESOURCES
Manufacturing
General farming
Dairy farming
Forest
Fruits and vegetables
Cattle, sheep, and hogs
Wheat and grain
Coal
Iron
Oil or natural gas
Limestone
Gold
Granite
Zinc
Lead
CANADA
Lake Superior
Lake Michigan
Lake Huron
Lake Erie
ND
Bismarck
MN
Minneapolis
SD
Sioux Falls
WI
Milwaukee
MI
Grand Rapids
Saginaw
Flint
Detroit
Toledo
Cleveland
Akron
IA
Des Moines
Omaha
NE
Chicago
IL
IN
OH
Columbus
Indianapolis
Dayton
Cincinnati
WV
CO
KS
Kansas City
Kansas City
St. Louis
MO
Evansville
KY
OK
AR
TN
0 100 200 Miles
0 100 200 Kilometers
Albers Equal-Area Projection

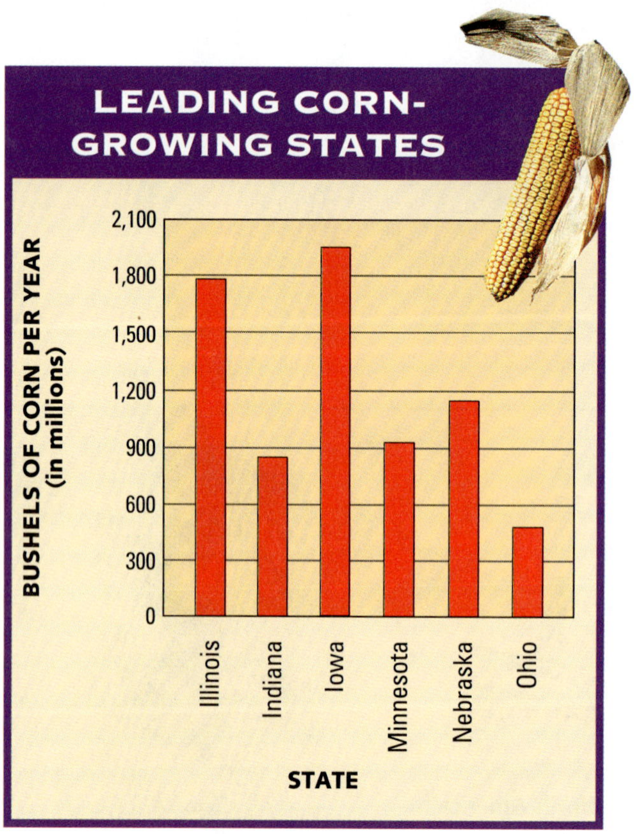
LEADING CORN-GROWING STATES
BUSHELS OF CORN PER YEAR (in millions)
2,100
1,800
1,500
1,200
900
600
300
0
Illinois
Indiana
Iowa
Minnesota
Nebraska
Ohio
STATE

PORTS ALONG THE GREAT LAKES

SOME WHEAT-GROWING STATES

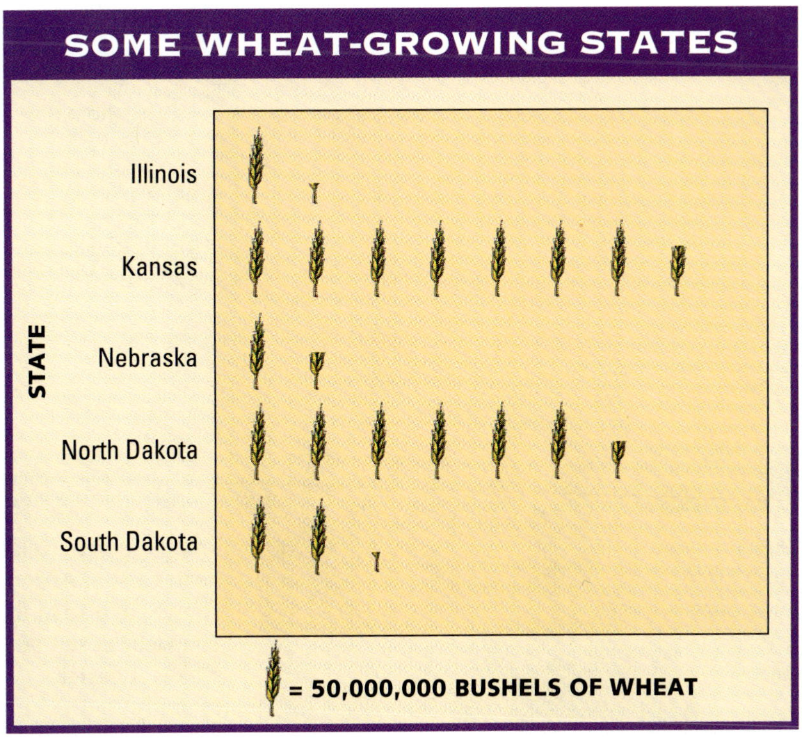

THE SOUTHWEST

REGION

Did You Know?

The Southwest region is made up of four large states—Arizona, New Mexico, Oklahoma, and Texas. It stretches west from the Gulf Coast of Texas to the Colorado River in Arizona. Mexico borders the region on the south.

THE SOUTHWEST STATES

STATE	CAPITAL	NICKNAME	POPULATION*
Arizona (AZ)	Phoenix	Grand Canyon State	4,223,000
New Mexico (NM)	Santa Fe	Land of Enchantment	1,737,000
Oklahoma (OK)	Oklahoma City	Sooner State	3,313,000
Texas (TX)	Austin	Lone Star State	19,180,000

*The most recent figures available.

TEN LARGEST CITIES

1. Houston, Texas
2. Dallas, Texas
3. Phoenix, Arizona
4. San Antonio, Texas
5. El Paso, Texas
6. Austin, Texas
7. Fort Worth, Texas
8. Oklahoma City, Oklahoma
9. Tucson, Arizona
10. Albuquerque, New Mexico

LEADING PRODUCTS AND RESOURCES

Farming: Beef cattle, citrus fruits, cotton, dairy cows, grain sorghum, hay, melons, rice, sheep, vegetables, wheat
Fishing: Crabs, fish, oysters, shrimp
Manufacturing: Chemicals, dairy products, electrical equipment, machinery, metal products, petroleum products, processed foods
Mining: Coal, copper, natural gas, oil, potash, silver,

One desert plant, an agave (uh•GAH•vee), lives from 10 to 15 years. Then it blooms once and dies. When it starts to bloom, the plant's stalk can grow as much as 16 inches (41 cm) in 24 hours.

There are more telescopes near Tucson, Arizona, than anywhere else in the world. The clear desert air there makes it easier to study the stars.

THE SOUTHWEST

There was a real Smokey Bear. He was a brown bear cub rescued from a forest fire in New Mexico's Lincoln National Forest. Today a state park in New Mexico is named for him.

The Four Corners is the only place in the United States where four states meet at a single point. The states are Arizona, Colorado, New Mexico, and Utah.

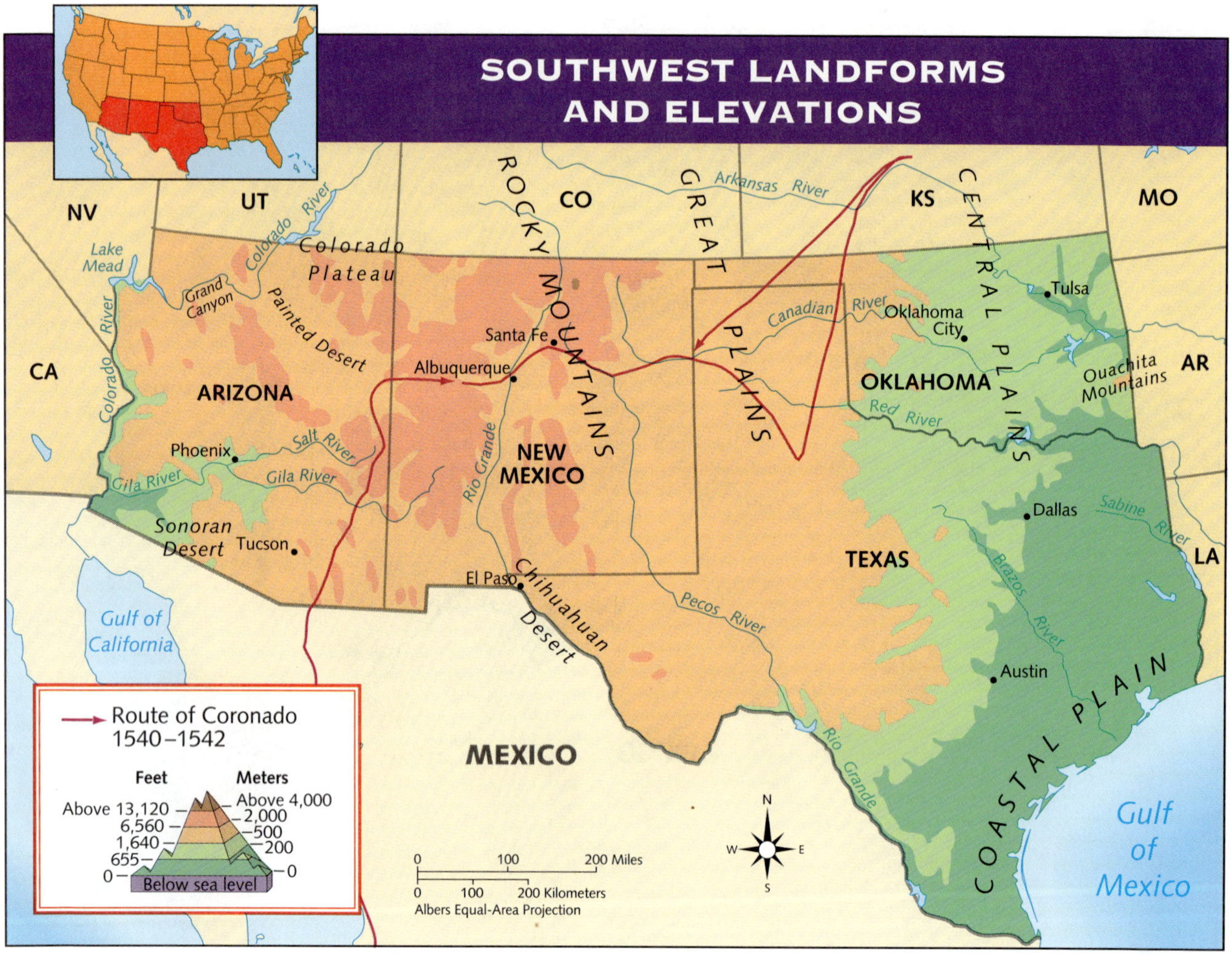

SOUTHWEST LANDFORMS AND ELEVATIONS
NV
UT
CO
KS
MO
CA
AR
LA
ARIZONA
NEW MEXICO
OKLAHOMA
TEXAS
MEXICO
ROCKY MOUNTAINS
GREAT PLAINS
CENTRAL PLAINS
COASTAL PLAIN
Colorado Plateau
Grand Canyon
Painted Desert
Sonoran Desert
Chihuahuan Desert
Ouachita Mountains
Lake Mead
Colorado River
Arkansas River
Canadian River
Red River
Salt River
Gila River
Rio Grande
Pecos River
Brazos River
Sabine River
Gulf of California
Gulf of Mexico
Santa Fe
Albuquerque
Phoenix
Tucson
El Paso
Oklahoma City
Tulsa
Dallas
Austin
Route of Coronado 1540–1542
Feet
Meters
Above 13,120
6,560
1,640
655
0
Above 4,000
2,000
500
200
0
Below sea level
0 100 200 Miles
0 100 200 Kilometers
Albers Equal-Area Projection
N
S
E
W

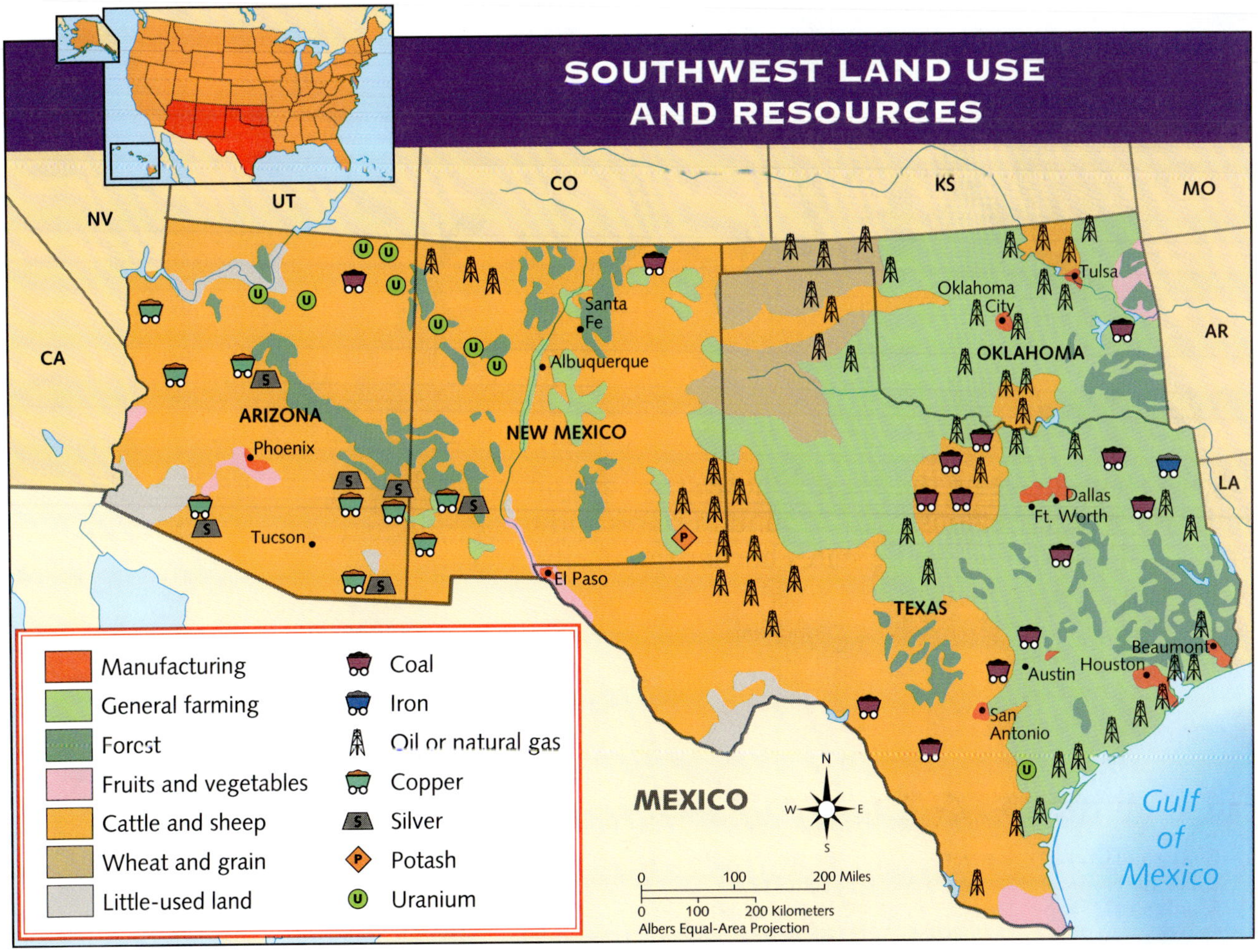
SOUTHWEST LAND USE AND RESOURCES
NV
UT
CO
KS
MO
CA
AR
LA
ARIZONA
NEW MEXICO
OKLAHOMA
TEXAS
MEXICO
Santa Fe
Albuquerque
Phoenix
Tucson
El Paso
Oklahoma City
Tulsa
Dallas
Ft. Worth
Austin
San Antonio
Houston
Beaumont
Gulf of Mexico
Manufacturing
General farming
Forest
Fruits and vegetables
Cattle and sheep
Wheat and grain
Little-used land
Coal
Iron
Oil or natural gas
Copper
Silver
Potash
Uranium
N
S
E
W
0 100 200 Miles
0 100 200 Kilometers
Albers Equal-Area Projection

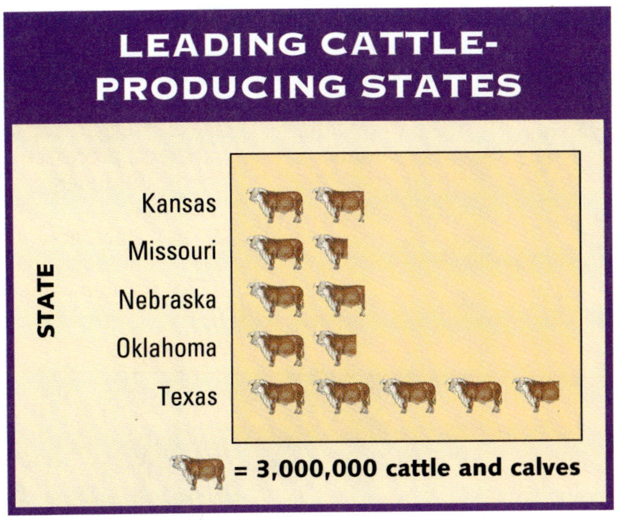
LEADING CATTLE-PRODUCING STATES
STATE
Kansas
Missouri
Nebraska
Oklahoma
Texas
= 3,000,000 cattle and calves

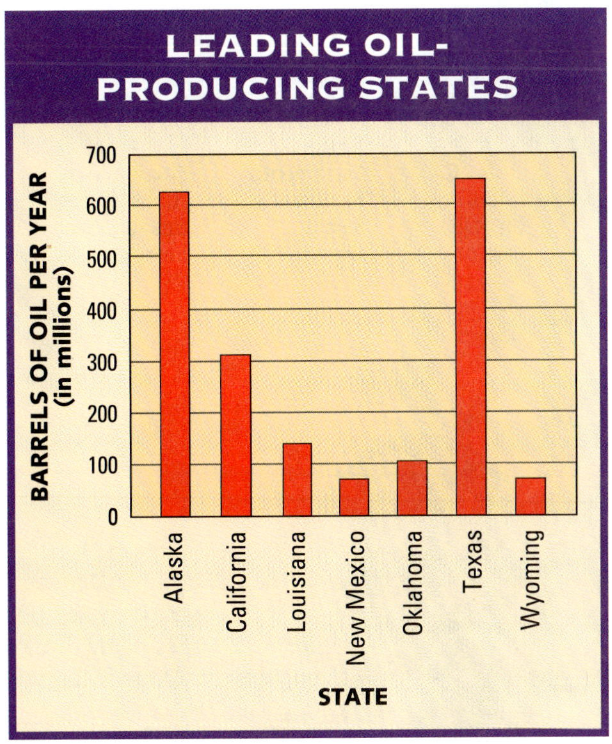
LEADING OIL-PRODUCING STATES
BARRELS OF OIL PER YEAR (in millions)
0
100
200
300
400
500
600
700
Alaska
California
Louisiana
New Mexico
Oklahoma
Texas
Wyoming
STATE

THE WEST

REGION

Did You Know?

Eleven states make up the West. Those states are often divided into two smaller regions—the Mountain states and the Pacific states. All five of the Pacific states border the Pacific Ocean.

STATE	CAPITAL	NICKNAME	POPULATION*
THE MOUNTAIN STATES			
Colorado (CO)	Denver	Centennial State	3,861,000
Idaho (ID)	Boise	Gem State	1,213,000
Montana (MT)	Helena	Treasure State	887,000
Nevada (NV)	Carson City	Silver State	1,571,000
Utah (UT)	Salt Lake City	Beehive State	2,030,000
Wyoming (WY)	Cheyenne	Equality State	501,000
THE PACIFIC STATES			
Alaska (AK)	Juneau	Last Frontier	663,000
California (CA)	Sacramento	Golden State	33,364,000
Hawaii (HI)	Honolulu	Aloha State	1,263,000
Oregon (OR)	Salem	Beaver State	3,249,000
Washington (WA)	Olympia	Evergreen State	5,735,000

*The most recent figures available.

TEN LARGEST CITIES

1. Los Angeles, California
2. San Diego, California
3. San Jose, California
4. San Francisco, California
5. Seattle, Washington
6. Denver, Colorado
7. Portland, Oregon
8. Long Beach, California
9. Sacramento, California
10. Fresno, California

LEADING PRODUCTS AND RESOURCES

Farming: Barley, beef cattle, coffee, cotton, dairy cows, fruits, hay, potatoes, rice, sheep, sugar beets, sugarcane, vegetables, wheat
Fishing: Crabs, fish, oysters, scallops, shrimp
Manufacturing: Chemicals, dairy products, electrical equipment, jet airplanes, lumber, metal products, paper products, processed foods, machinery
Mining: Coal, copper, gold, lead, natural gas, oil, silver, uranium, zinc

The U.S. Mint in Denver, Colorado, can make as many as 40 million coins a day. It makes many of the coins used throughout the United States.

Crater Lake, in Oregon, is the deepest lake in the United States. In one place it is 1,932 feet (589 m) deep.

THE WEST

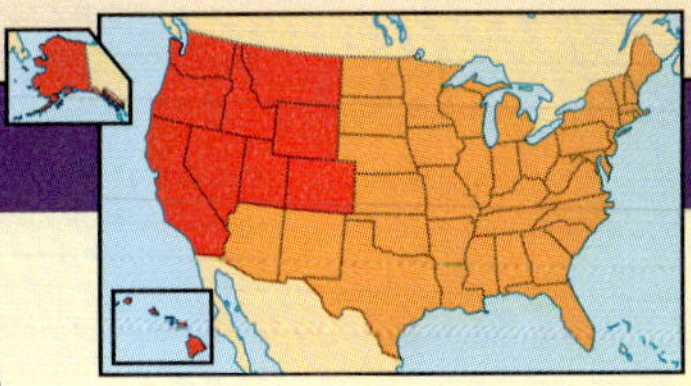

Yosemite Falls, in California, is 13 times higher than Niagara Falls.

More bald eagles gather along the Chilkat River, in Alaska, than at any other place in the world. They fly there to catch salmon from the river.

LANDFORMS AND ELEVATIONS IN THE WEST

ALASKA

HAWAII

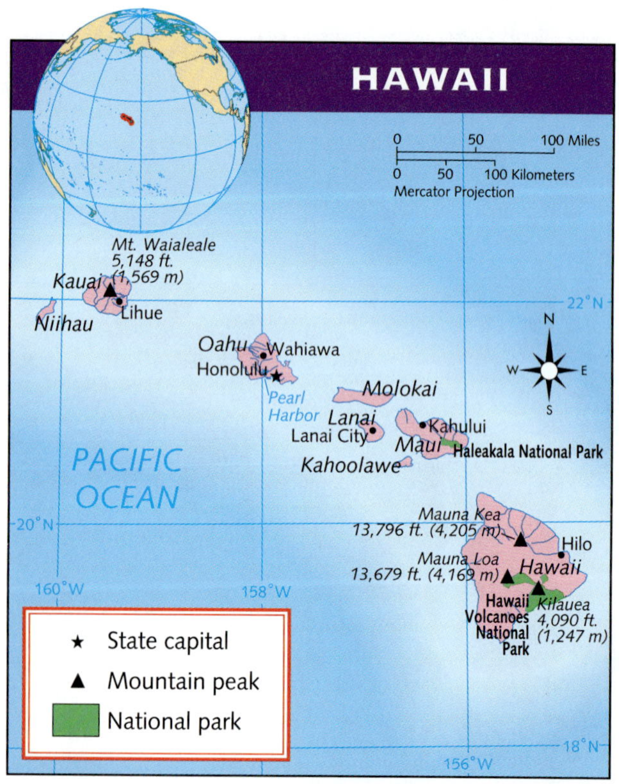

THE PACIFIC NORTHWEST

GUAM

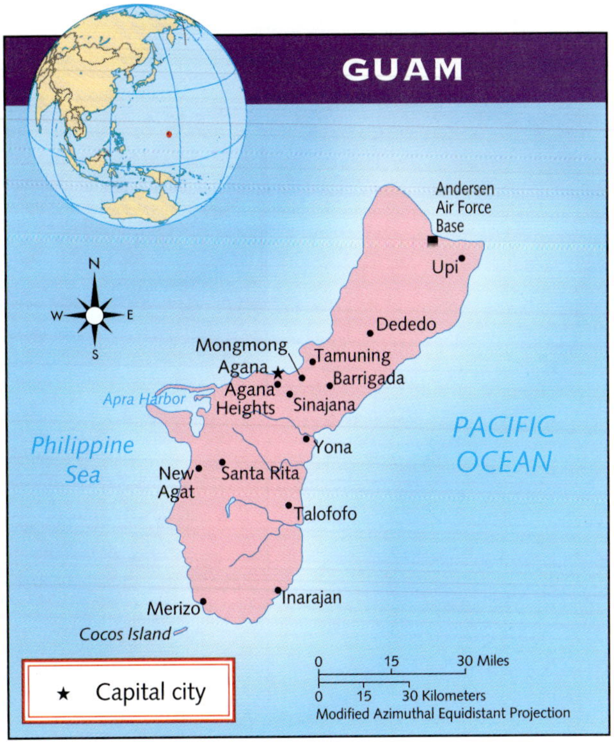

AVERAGE HEIGHT OF THREE KINDS OF TREES

INSIDE A VOLCANO

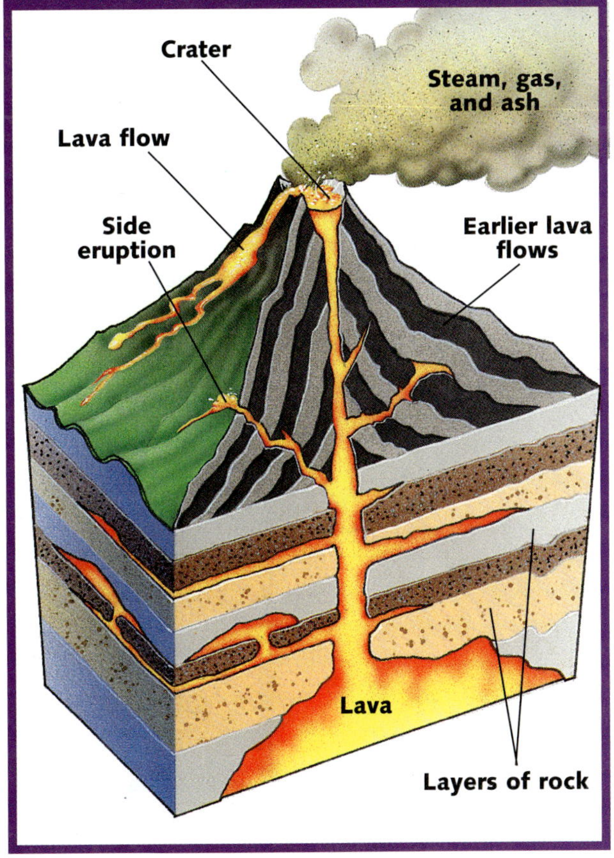

POPULATION MAP OF CALIFORNIA, OREGON, AND WASHINGTON

LAND USE AND RESOURCES IN THE WEST

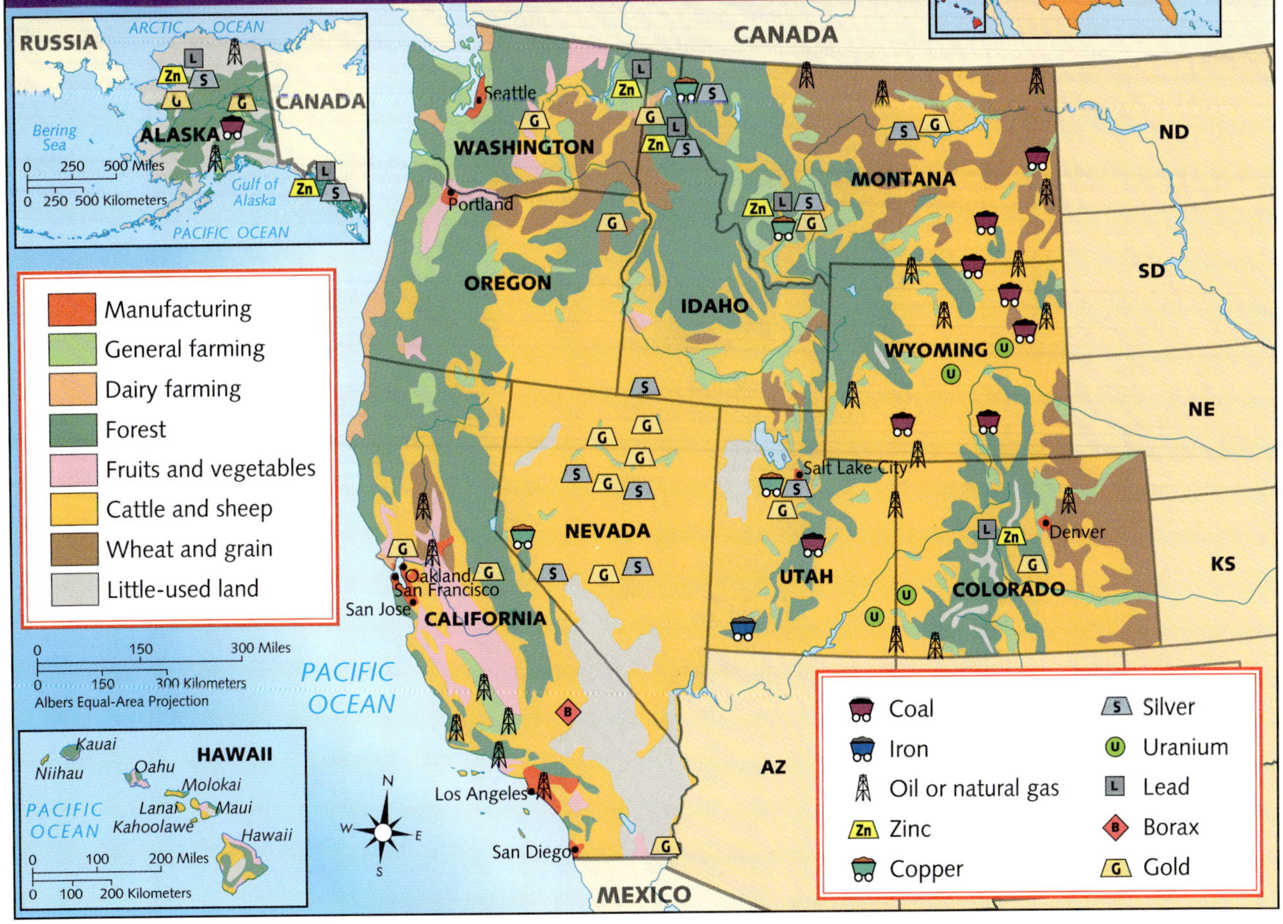

LEADING MANUFACTURING STATES

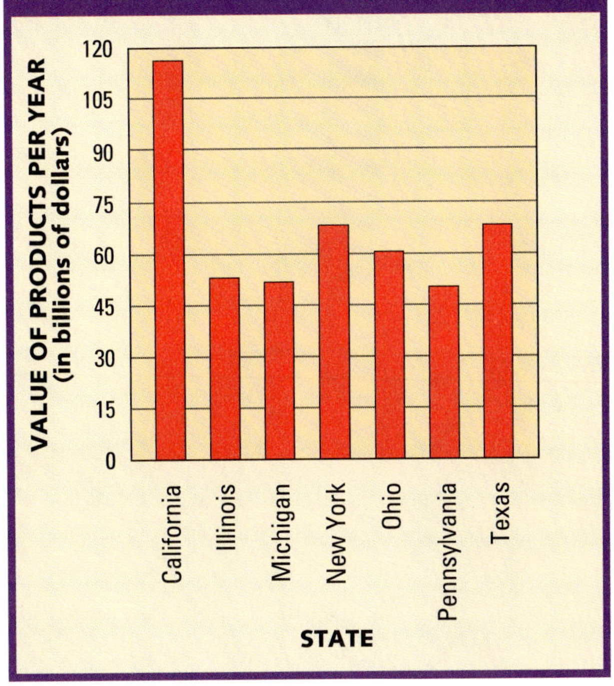

ALMANAC

ALMANAC

FACTS ABOUT THE WORLD

Country	Capital	Population*	Area (sq. mi.)	Economy
Africa				
Algeria	Algiers	27,895,000	919,595	oil, light industry, food processing
Angola	Luanda	9,804,000	481,354	textiles, coffee, bananas, iron, diamonds
Benin	Porto-Novo	5,342,000	43,500	palm products, peanuts, cotton, coffee, oil
Botswana	Gaborone	1,359,000	224,607	livestock processing, corn, coal, big game
Burkina Faso	Ouagadougou	10,135,000	105,946	grain, manganese, gold
Burundi	Bujumbura	6,125,000	10,740	coffee, cotton, tea
Cameroon	Yaoundé	13,132,000	183,569	aluminum, oil products, palm products, cocoa, coffee, timber
Cape Verde	Praia	423,000	1,557	bananas, coffee, beets, salt
Central African Republic	Bangui	3,142,000	240,324	textiles, cotton, coffee, diamonds
Chad	N'Djamena	5,467,000	495,755	cotton, uranium, fish
Comoro Islands	Moroni	530,000	719	perfume, vanilla, copra, plants, fruits
Congo	Brazzaville	2,447,000	132,047	palm oil, cocoa, coffee, tobacco, gold
Djibouti	Djibouti	413,000	8,950	salt
Egypt	Cairo	59,325,000	385,229	textiles, chemicals, cotton, rice, beans, oil
Equatorial Guinea	Malabo	410,000	10,831	cocoa, coffee, bananas, sweet potatoes, timber
Eritrea	Asmara	3,200,000	45,300	cotton, coffee, tobacco
Ethiopia	Addis Ababa	58,710,000	437,794	cement, textiles, coffee, grain, platinum, gold
Gabon	Libreville	1,139,000	103,347	cocoa, coffee, manganese, uranium, oil
Gambia	Banjul	959,000	4,127	tourism, peanuts, rice, fish
Ghana	Accra	17,225,000	92,098	aluminum, cocoa, gold, manganese
Guinea	Conakry	6,392,000	94,926	bananas, pineapples, iron, diamonds
Guinea-Bissau	Bissau	1,098,000	13,948	peanuts, cotton, rice, bauxite
Ivory Coast (Côte d'Ivoire)	Yamoussoukro	14,296,000	124,504	coffee, cocoa, diamonds, timber, rubber
Kenya	Nairobi	28,241,000	224,961	tourism, coffee, corn, gold
Lesotho	Maseru	1,944,000	11,716	corn, grain, peas, beans, diamonds
Liberia	Monrovia	2,973,000	38,250	mining, rice, cassava, coffee, iron, diamonds, gold, rubber, timber
Libya	Tripoli	5,057,000	679,359	carpets, textiles, petroleum, dates, olives, gypsum, oil, gas
Madagascar	Antananarivo	13,428,000	226,658	textiles, coffee, cloves, vanilla, chromium, graphite
Malawi	Lilongwe	9,732,000	45,747	textiles, sugar, cement, tea, tobacco, coffee, rubber
Mali	Bamako	9,113,000	482,077	millet, rice, peanuts, cotton, bauxite, iron, gold
Mauritania	Nouakchott	2,193,000	398,000	dates, grain, iron ore, gypsum
Mauritius	Port Louis	1,117,000	788	tourism, sugarcane, tea
Morocco	Rabat	28,559,000	177,117	carpets, clothing, leather goods, grain, fruits, copper, cobalt

Country	Capital	Population*	Area (sq. mi.)	Economy
Mozambique	Maputo	17,346,000	313,661	cement, alcohol, textiles, cashews, cotton, sugar, coal, titanium
Namibia	Windhoek	1,596,000	318,146	diamonds, sheep, cattle, fish
Niger	Niamey	8,635,000	497,000	peanuts, cotton, uranium, coal, iron
Nigeria	Abuja	98,091,000	356,669	textiles, cocoa, tobacco, oil, gas
Rwanda	Kigali	8,374,000	10,169	coffee, tea, tin
São Tomé and Príncipe	São Tomé	137,000	386	cocoa, coconut
Senegal	Dakar	8,731,000	75,951	food processing, fishing, peanuts, phosphates
Seychelles	Victoria	72,000	176	food processing, coconut products, cinnamon, vanilla
Sierra Leone	Freetown	4,630,000	27,699	mining, tourism, cocoa, coffee, diamonds
Somalia	Mogadishu	6,667,000	246,300	incense, sugar, bananas, iron, tin
South Africa	Cape Town	43,931,000	473,290	steel, tires, corn, wool, gold, diamonds
Sudan	Khartoum	29,420,000	966,757	gum arabic, cotton, sesame, peanuts, chrome, mahogany
Swaziland	Mbabane	936,000	6,704	wood pulp, sugar, corn, cotton, asbestos
Tanzania	Dar es Salaam	27,986,000	364,017	food processing, clothing, cotton, diamonds, hides
Togo	Lomé	4,255,000	21,925	textiles, shoes, coffee, cocoa, yams, phosphates
Tunisia	Tunis	8,727,000	63,378	textiles, oil products, grain, olives, citrus fruits, figs, phosphates
Uganda	Kampala	19,859,000	93,070	coffee, cotton, tea, copper, cobalt
Zaire	Kinshasa	42,684,000	905,446	coffee, rice, sugar cane, cobalt, copper
Zambia	Lusaka	9,188,000	290,586	corn, tobacco, peanuts, cobalt, rubber, ivory
Zimbabwe	Harare	10,975,000	150,872	clothing, chemicals, tobacco, sugar, cotton, chromium, gold
Asia				
Afghanistan	Kabul	16,903,000	251,825	textiles, furniture, fruits, copper, coal, wool
Armenia	Yerevan	3,522,000	11,500	mining, cotton, figs, copper
Azerbaijan	Baku	7,684,000	33,400	oil, grain, cotton, iron, cattle
Bahrain	Manama	586,000	268	oil products, aluminum
Bangladesh	Dhaka	125,149,000	57,295	jute, textiles, fertilizers, rice, tea
Bhutan	Thimphu	1,739,000	18,147	handicrafts, rice, corn, timber
Brunei	Bandar Seri Begawan	285,000	2,226	petroleum, rice, bananas, cassava
Burma (Myanmar)	Rangoon (Yangôn)	44,277,000	261,228	textiles, petroleum, rice, sugar cane, lead, silver, precious stones
Cambodia	Phnom Penh	10,265,000	70,238	rice, wood, rubber, corn
China	Beijing	1,190,431,000	3,696,100	iron, steel, textiles, grain, rice, cotton, tea
Cyprus	Nicosia	730,000	3,572	grains, carobs, citrus fruits, olives, copper
Georgia	Tbilisi	5,681,000	26,900	manganese, citrus fruits, wheat, grapes
India	New Delhi	919,903,000	1,222,559	textiles, steel, rice, grain, coffee, spices, coal

*These population figures are from the most recent available statistics.

Country	Capital	Population*	Area (sq. mi.)	Economy
Indonesia	Jakarta	200,410,000	741,052	textiles, rice, coffee, sugar, nickel, tin, rubber
Iran	Tehran	65,612,000	632,457	cement, sugar refining, carpets, grain, rice, oil, gas
Iraq	Baghdad	19,890,000	167,975	textiles, cement, dates, oil
Israel	Jerusalem	5,051,000	7,992	diamond cutting, textiles, electronics, citrus fruit, potash
Japan	Tokyo	125,107,000	145,850	electronics, autos, rice, grain
Jordan	Amman	3,961,000	34,342	textiles, cement, grain, olives, phosphate
Kazakhstan	Almaty	17,268,000	1,049,200	steel, cement, footwear, grain, cotton
Kuwait	Kuwait City	1,819,000	6,880	oil, oil products, gas
Kyrgyzstan	Bishkek	4,698,000	76,642	tobacco, textiles, mining, wheat, sugar beets
Laos	Vientiane	4,702,000	91,429	wood products, mining, rice, corn, tobacco,
Lebanon	Beirut	3,620,000	3,950	textiles, oil products, fruits, olives, vegetables
Malaysia	Kuala Lumpur	19,283,000	127,584	rubber goods, steel, electronics, palm oil, copra, tin, iron
Maldives	Male	252,000	115	fish processing, tourism, coconuts, fruit, millet, shells
Mongolia	Ulaanbaatar	2,430,000	604,800	textiles, chemicals, grain, coal, copper
Nepal	Kathmandu	21,042,000	56,827	sugar, jute, tourism, rice, grain
North Korea	P'yongyang	23,067,000	47,399	textiles, corn, potatoes
Oman	Muscat	1,701,000	118,150	fruits, quartz, vegetables, wheat, oil
Pakistan	Islamabad	121,856,000	339,697	textiles, chemicals, petroleum products, rice, wheat, natural gas, iron ore, wool
Philippines	Manila	69,809,000	115,860	textiles, clothing, wood products, sugar, cobalt, copper
Qatar	Doha	513,000	4,412	oil, petroleum products
Saudi Arabia	Riyadh	18,197,000	865,000	oil products, dates, wheat, oil, gas
Singapore	Singapore	2,859,000	247	shipbuilding, oil refining, electronics, banking, tourism
South Korea	Seoul	45,083,000	38,330	electronics, textiles, clothing, motor vehicles, rice, barley
Sri Lanka	Colombo	18,033,000	25,332	plywood, paper, tea, coconuts, rice, graphite, gems
Syria	Damascus	14,887,000	71,498	oil products, textiles, cotton, grain, olives
Taiwan	Taipei	21,299,000	13,969	textiles, clothing, electronics, rice, bananas, coal, marble
Tajikistan	Dushanbe	5,995,000	55,300	cement, barley, coal, lead
Thailand	Bangkok	59,510,000	198,115	tourism, rice, corn, tapioca, sugar cane
Turkey	Ankara	62,154,000	300,948	iron, steel, tobacco, grain, mercury
Turkmenistan	Ashgabat	3,995,000	188,417	mining, textiles, grain, cotton, coal, sulfur, salt
United Arab Emirates	Abu Dhabi	2,791,000	30,000	vegetables, dates, limes, oil
Uzbekistan	Tashkent	22,609,000	172,700	steel, tractors, cotton, coal
Vietnam	Hanoi	73,104,000	127,246	food processing, textiles, rice, rubber, phosphates
Yemen	Sanaa	11,105,000	205,356	mining, petroleum refining, wheat, sorghum, salt

Country	Capital	Population*	Area (sq. mi.)	Economy
Australia and Oceania				
Australia	Canberra	18,077,000	2,966,200	iron, textiles, electrical equipment, wheat, coal
Fiji	Suva	764,000	7,056	tourism, sugar, bananas, gold
Kiribati	Tarawa	78,000	313	copra, coconuts, breadfruit, bananas, fish
Marshall Islands	Majuro	54,000	70	agriculture, tourism
Micronesia	Palikir	120,000	271	tropical fruits, vegetables, coconuts
Nauru	Yaren	10,000	8	phosphate mining, coconuts
New Zealand	Wellington	3,389,000	104,454	textiles, machinery, fish, forest products, grain, fruits, oil, gas
Papua New Guinea	Port Moresby	4,197,000	178,704	coffee, coconuts, cocoa, gold, copper, silver
Solomon Islands	Honiara	386,000	10,954	fish canning, coconuts, rice
Tonga	Nuku'alofa	105,000	301	tourism, coconut products, bananas
Tuvalu	Funafuti	10,000	9	copra, coconuts
Vanuatu	Portvila	170,000	4,707	fish freezing, meat canneries, tourism, copra
Western Samoa	Apia	204,000	1,093	cocoa, copra, bananas, hardwoods, fish
Europe				
Albania	Tiranë	3,374,000	11,100	cement, textiles, food processing, corn, wheat
Andorra	Andorra la Vella	64,000	181	tourism, tobacco products, commerce, services
Austria	Vienna	7,955,000	32,378	steel, machinery, autos, grain, iron ore
Belarus	Minsk	10,405,000	80,134	food processing, chemicals, grain, potatoes, sugar beets
Belgium	Brussels	10,063,000	11,787	steel, diamond cutting, wheat, coal
Bosnia and Herzegovina	Sarajevo	4,651,000	19,741	textiles, carpets, timber, corn, bauxite
Bulgaria	Sofia	8,800,000	42,855	chemicals, machinery, metals, textiles
Croatia	Zagreb	4,698,000	21,829	textiles, chemicals, olives, bauxite
Czech Republic	Prague	10,408,000	30,449	machinery, oil products, chemicals, wheat, sugar beets
Denmark	Copenhagen	5,188,000	16,639	machinery, textiles, furniture, dairy products
Estonia	Tallinn	1,617,000	17,413	agricultural machinery, grain, vegetables
Finland	Helsinki	5,069,000	130,559	machinery, metal, shipbuilding, grain, potatoes, copper
France	Paris	57,840,000	210,026	steel, textiles, wine, perfume, grain, fruits, vegetables
Germany	Berlin	81,088,000	137,735	steel, ships, motor vehicles, grain, potatoes, coal
Greece	Athens	10,565,000	50,949	textiles, chemicals, wine, grain, olives, citrus fruits, bauxite
Hungary	Budapest	10,319,000	35,919	iron, steel, pharmaceuticals, grain, bauxite, coal
Iceland	Reykjavik	264,000	36,699	fish products, aluminum, potatoes

*These population figures are from the most recent available statistics.

Country	Capital	Population*	Area (sq. mi.)	Economy
Ireland	Dublin	3,539,000	27,137	textiles, chemicals, brewing, tourism, potatoes, grain, zinc
Italy	Rome	58,138,000	116,333	steel, machinery, autos, textiles, shoes, grapes, olives
Latvia	Riga	2,749,000	24,900	railway cars, paper, oats, barley, potatoes
Liechtenstein	Vaduz	30,000	62	machines, instruments, chemicals, furniture, ceramics
Lithuania	Vilnius	3,848,000	25,213	shipbuilding, grain, potatoes, vegetables
Luxembourg	Luxembourg	402,000	999	steel, chemicals, beer, corn, wine, iron
Macedonia	Skopje	2,214,000	9,928	steel, cement, wheat, cotton, tobacco
Malta	Valletta	367,000	122	textiles, tourism, potatoes, tomatoes
Moldova	Chisinau	4,473,000	13,012	wine, textiles, grain, lignite, gypsum
Monaco	Monaco	31,000	0.75	tourism, chemicals, plastics
Netherlands	Amsterdam	15,368,000	16,033	metals, machinery, chemicals, grain, potatoes, flowers, natural gas, oil
Norway	Oslo	4,315,000	125,050	paper, shipbuilding, grain, potatoes, oil, copper
Poland	Warsaw	38,655,000	120,727	shipbuilding, chemicals, grain, potatoes, sugar beets, coal
Portugal	Lisbon	10,524,000	35,672	textiles, footwear, cork, grain, potatoes
Romania	Bucharest	23,181,000	91,699	steel, metals, textiles, grain, oil
Russia**	Moscow	149,609,000	6,592,800	steel, machinery, motor vehicles, chemicals, cement, grain, sugar beets
San Marino	San Marino	24,000	24	postage stamps, tourism, woolen goods
Slovakia	Bratislava	5,404,000	18,933	iron, steel, glass, wheat, potatoes
Slovenia	Ljubljana	1,972,000	7,821	steel, textiles, coal, mercury, wheat, potatoes
Spain	Madrid	39,303,000	194,898	machinery, grain, olives, lignite, uranium, cork
Sweden	Stockholm	8,778,000	173,732	steel, machinery, automobiles, grain, potatoes, zinc, iron
Switzerland	Bern and Lausanne	7,040,000	15,943	instruments, watches, food, banking, tourism
Ukraine	Kiev	51,847,000	233,100	steel, chemicals, grain, sugar beets, potatoes, iron, manganese
United Kingdom	London	58,135,000	94,251	steel, motor vehicles, shipbuilding, banking, grain, sugar beets, coal, tin
Vatican City	none	811	.17	tourism, postage stamps
Yugoslavia	Belgrade	10,760,000	39,449	steel, wood products, corn, grain
North and Central America				
Antigua and Barbuda	St. John's	65,000	171	manufacturing, tourism
Bahamas	Nassau	273,000	5,382	tourism, rum, banking
Barbados	Bridgetown	256,000	166	sugar, tourism
Belize	Belmopan	209,000	8,867	sugar
Canada	Ottawa	28,114,000	3,849,674	nickel, zinc, copper, gold, livestock, fish
Costa Rica	San José	3,342,000	19,730	furniture, aluminum, textiles, fertilizers, coffee, gold

**in both Asia and Europe

Country	Capital	Population*	Area (sq. mi.)	Economy
Cuba	Havana	11,064,000	42,804	cement, sugar, tobacco, rice, coffee
Dominica	Roseau	88,000	290	tourism, bananas, pumice
Dominican Republic	Santo Domingo	7,826,000	18,704	sugar, cement, cocoa, coffee
El Salvador	San Salvador	5,753,000	8,124	food products, textiles, petroleum, coffee
Greenland	Nuuk	57,000	840,000	fish
Grenada	St. George's	94,000	133	rum, nutmeg, bananas, cocoa
Guatemala	Guatemala City	10,721,000	42,042	tires, textiles, coffee, sugar, bananas, oil
Haiti	Port-au-Prince	6,491,000	10,695	textiles, coffee, sugar, bananas, bauxite, timber
Honduras	Tegucigalpa	5,315,000	43,277	textiles, wood products, bananas, coffee, gold, silver
Jamaica	Kingston	2,555,000	4,244	rum, molasses, tourism, sugar cane, coffee, bananas, bauxite
Mexico	Mexico City	92,202,000	756,066	steel, chemicals, textiles, rubber, petroleum, tourism, cotton, coffee, silver, lead, natural gas
Nicaragua	Managua	4,097,000	50,880	chemicals, textiles, cotton, fruit, yucca, coffee, gold, silver
Panama	Panama City	2,630,000	29,157	oil refining, international banking, bananas, copper, mahogany
Saint Kitts and Nevis	Basseterre	41,000	104	sugar
Trinidad and Tobago	Port-of-Spain	1,328,000	1,980	oil products, rum, cement, tourism, sugar, cocoa, asphalt
United States of America	Washington, D.C.	260,714,000	3,787,318	coal, electronics, machinery, computers, wheat
South America				
Argentina	Buenos Aires	33,913,000	1,073,518	food processing, chemicals, grain, oil
Bolivia	La Paz/Sucre	7,719,000	424,164	textiles, mining, potatoes, sugar, coffee, tin
Brazil	Brasília	158,739,000	3,286,470	steel, automobiles, ships, coffee
Chile	Santiago	13,951,000	292,135	fish, wood, grain, copper
Colombia	Bogota	35,578,000	440,831	textiles, chemicals, coffee, emeralds
Ecuador	Quito	10,677,000	105,037	wood, textiles, bananas, coffee, rice, oil
Guyana	Georgetown	729,000	83,044	mining, textiles, sugar, bauxite, diamonds
Netherlands Antilles	Willemstad	184,000	385	oil, tourism, shipbuilding
Paraguay	Asunción	5,214,000	157,048	wood products, textiles, cement, corn, cotton, iron
Peru	Lima	23,651,000	496,225	fish meal, textiles, cotton, copper, wool
Saint Vincent and the Grenadines	Kingstown	115,000	150	tourism, bananas, arrowroot, coconuts
Suriname	Paramaribo	423,000	63,251	rice, sugar, fruits, bauxite
Uruguay	Montevideo	3,199,000	68,037	meatpacking, textiles, wine, oil products, corn, wheat
Venezuela	Caracas	20,562,000	352,144	textiles, paper, coffee, rice, oil, iron

*These population figures are from the most recent available statistics.

ALMANAC

FACTS ABOUT THE STATES

State	Year of Statehood	Population*	Area (sq. mi.)	Capital	Origin of State Name
Alabama	1819	4,361,000	51,609	Montgomery	Choctaw, *alba ayamule,* "one who clears land and gathers food from it"
Alaska	1959	663,000	586,412	Juneau	Aleut, *alayeska,* "great land"
Arizona	1912	4,223,000	113,909	Phoenix	Papago, *arizonac,* "place of the small spring"
Arkansas	1836	2,513,000	53,104	Little Rock	Quapaw, "the downstream people"
California	1850	33,364,000	158,693	Sacramento	Spanish, "an early paradise"
Colorado	1876	3,861,000	104,247	Denver	Spanish, "red land" or "red earth"
Connecticut	1788	3,268,000	5,009	Hartford	Mohican, *quinnitukqut,* "at the long tidal river"
Delaware	1787	736,000	2,057	Dover	Named for Lord de la Warr
Florida	1845	14,663,000	58,560	Tallahassee	Spanish, "land of flowers"
Georgia	1788	7,324,000	58,876	Atlanta	Named for King George II of England
Hawaii	1959	1,263,000	6,450	Honolulu	Polynesian, *hawaiki* or *owykee,* "homeland"
Idaho	1890	1,213,000	83,557	Boise	Shoshone, "light on the mountains"
Illinois	1818	11,989,000	56,400	Springfield	Algonquian, *iliniwek,* "men" or "warriors"
Indiana	1816	5,920,000	36,291	Indianapolis	*Indian* + a = "land of the Indians"
Iowa	1846	2,893,000	56,290	Des Moines	Dakota, *ayuba,* "beautiful land"
Kansas	1861	2,652,000	82,264	Topeka	Sioux, "land of the south wind people"
Kentucky	1792	3,911, 000	40,395	Frankfort	Cherokee, *Kentake,* "meadowland"
Louisiana	1812	4,404,000	48,523	Baton Rouge	Named for King Louis XIV of France
Maine	1820	1,236, 000	33,215	Augusta	Named after a French province
Maryland	1788	5,180,000	10,577	Annapolis	Named for Henrietta Maria, Queen Consort of Charles I of England
Massachusetts	1788	5,959,000	8,257	Boston	Algonquian, "at the big hill" or "place of the big hill"
Michigan	1837	9,656,000	58,216	Lansing	Chippewa, *mica gama,* "big water"
Minnesota	1858	4,706, 000	84,068	St. Paul	Dakota Sioux, "sky-blue water"
Mississippi	1817	2,700,000	47,716	Jackson	Chippewa, *mici sibi,* "big river"
Missouri	1821	5,347,000	69,686	Jefferson City	Algonquian,"muddy water"or "people of the big canoes"
Montana	1889	887,000	147,138	Helena	Spanish, "mountainous"
Nebraska	1867	1,639,000	77,227	Lincoln	Omaha, *ni-bthaska,* "river in the flatness"

State	Year of Statehood	Population*	Area (sq. mi.)	Capital	Origin of State Name
Nevada	1864	1,499,000	110,540	Carson City	Spanish, "snowy" or "snowed upon"
New Hampshire	1788	1,144,000	9,304	Concord	Named for Hampshire County, England
New Jersey	1787	8,015,000	7,836	Trenton	Named for the Isle of Jersey
New Mexico	1912	1,737,000	121,666	Santa Fe	Named by Spanish explorers from Mexico
New York	1788	18,198,000	49,576	Albany	Named after the Duke of York
North Carolina	1789	7,347,000	52,586	Raleigh	Named after King Charles II of England
North Dakota	1889	639,000	70,665	Bismarck	Sioux, *dakota,* "friend" or "ally"
Ohio	1803	11,318,000	41,222	Columbus	Iroquois, *oheo,* "beautiful, beautiful water"
Oklahoma	1907	3,313,000	69,919	Oklahoma City	Choctaw, "red people"
Oregon	1859	3,249,000	96,981	Salem	Algonquian, *wauregan,* "beautiful water"
Pennsylvania	1787	12,210,000	45,333	Harrisburg	*Penn + sylvania,* meaning "Penn's woods"
Rhode Island	1790	998,000	1,214	Providence	Dutch, "red-clay island"
South Carolina	1788	3,814,000	31,055	Columbia	Named after King Charles II of England
South Dakota	1889	750,000	77,047	Pierre	Sioux, *dakota,* "friend" or "ally"
Tennessee	1796	5,359,000	42,244	Nashville	Name of a Cherokee village
Texas	1845	19,180,000	267,338	Austin	Indian, *tejas* "friend" or "ally"
Utah	1896	2,030,000	84,916	Salt Lake City	Ute, "land of the Ute"
Vermont	1791	584,000	9,609	Montpelier	French, *vert,* "green" and *mont,* "mountain"
Virginia	1788	6,814,000	40,817	Richmond	Named after Queen Elizabeth I of England
Washington	1889	5,735,000	68,192	Olympia	Named for George Washington
West Virginia	1863	1,832,000	24,181	Charleston	From the English-named state of Virginia
Wisconsin	1848	5,256,000	56,154	Madison	Possibly Algonquian, "grassy place" or "place of the beaver"
Wyoming	1890	501,000	97,914	Cheyenne	Algonquian, *mache-weaming,* "at the big flats"
District of Columbia		545,000	67		Named after Christopher Columbus

*These population figures are from the most recent available statistics.

ALMANAC

FACTS ABOUT THE PRESIDENTS

George Washington 1732–1799

Birthplace: *Westmoreland County, VA*
Home State: *VA*
Political Party: *None*
Age at Inauguration: *57*
Served: *1789–1797*
Vice President: *John Adams*

John Adams 1735–1826

Birthplace: *Braintree, MA*
Home State: *MA*
Political Party: *Federalist*
Age at Inauguration: *61*
Served: *1797–1801*
Vice President: *Thomas Jefferson*

Thomas Jefferson 1743–1826

Birthplace: *Albemarle County, VA*
Home State: *VA*
Political Party: *Democratic-Republican*
Age at Inauguration: *57*
Served: *1801–1809*
Vice Presidents: *Aaron Burr, George Clinton*

James Madison 1751–1836

Birthplace: *Port Conway, VA*
Home State: *VA*
Political Party: *Democratic-Republican*
Age at Inauguration: *57*
Served: *1809–1817*
Vice Presidents: *George Clinton, Elbridge Gerry*

James Monroe 1758–1831

Birthplace: *Westmoreland County, VA*
Home State: *VA*
Political Party: *Democratic-Republican*
Age at Inauguration: *58*
Served: *1817–1825*
Vice President: *Daniel D. Tompkins*

John Quincy Adams 1767–1848

Birthplace: *Braintree, MA*
Home State: *MA*
Political Party: *Democratic-Republican*
Age at Inauguration: *57*
Served: *1825–1829*
Vice President: *John C. Calhoun*

Andrew Jackson 1767–1845

Birthplace: *Waxhaw settlement, SC*
Home State: *TN*
Political Party: *Democratic*
Age at Inauguration: *61*
Served: *1829–1837*
Vice Presidents: *John C. Calhoun, Martin Van Buren*

Martin Van Buren 1782–1862

Birthplace: *Kinderhook, NY*
Home State: *NY*
Political Party: *Democratic*
Age at Inauguration: *54*
Served: *1837–1841*
Vice President: *Richard M. Johnson*

William H. Harrison 1773–1841

Birthplace: *Berkeley, VA*
Home State: *OH*
Political Party: *Whig*
Age at Inauguration: *68*
Served: *1841*
Vice President: *John Tyler*

John Tyler 1790–1862

Birthplace: *Greenway, VA*
Home State: *VA*
Political Party: *Whig*
Age at Inauguration: *51*
Served: *1841–1845*
Vice President: *none*

James K. Polk 1795–1849

Birthplace: *near Pineville, NC*
Home State: *TN*
Political Party: *Democratic*
Age at Inauguration: *49*
Served: *1845–1849*
Vice President: *George M. Dallas*

Zachary Taylor 1784–1850

Birthplace: *Orange County, VA*
Home State: *LA*
Political Party: *Whig*
Age at Inauguration: *64*
Served: *1849–1850*
Vice President: *Millard Fillmore*

Birthplace: *Locke, NY*
Home State: *NY*
Political Party: *Whig*
Age at Inauguration: *50*
Served: *1850–1853*
Vice President: *none*

Millard Fillmore 1800–1874

Birthplace: *Hillsboro, NH*
Home State: *NH*
Political Party: *Democratic*
Age at Inauguration: *48*
Served: *1853–1857*
Vice President: *William R. King*

Franklin Pierce 1804–1869

Birthplace: *near Mercersburg, PA*
Home State: *PA*
Political Party: *Democratic*
Age at Inauguration: *65*
Served: *1857–1861*
Vice President: *John C. Breckinridge*

James Buchanan 1791–1868

Birthplace: *near Hodgenville, KY*
Home State: *IL*
Political Party: *Republican*
Age at Inauguration: *52*
Served: *1861–1865*
Vice Presidents: *Hannibal Hamlin, Andrew Johnson*

Abraham Lincoln 1809–1865

Birthplace: *Raleigh, NC*
Home State: *TN*
Political Party: *National Union*
Age at Inauguration: *56*
Served: *1865–1869*
Vice President: *none*

Andrew Johnson 1808–1875

Birthplace: *Point Pleasant, OH*
Home State: *IL*
Political Party: *Republican*
Age at Inauguration: *46*
Served: *1869–1877*
Vice Presidents: *Schuyler Colfax, Henry Wilson*

Ulysses S. Grant 1822–1885

Birthplace: *Delaware, OH*
Home State: *OH*
Political Party: *Republican*
Age at Inauguration: *54*
Served: *1877–1881*
Vice President: *William A. Wheeler*

Rutherford B. Hayes 1822–1893

Birthplace: *Orange, OH*
Home State: *OH*
Political Party: *Republican*
Age at Inauguration: *49*
Served: *1881*
Vice President: *Chester A. Arthur*

James A. Garfield 1831–1881

Birthplace: *Fairfield, VT*
Home State: *NY*
Political Party: *Republican*
Age at Inauguration: *51*
Served: *1881–1885*
Vice President: *none*

Chester A. Arthur 1829–1886

Birthplace: *Caldwell, NJ*
Home State: *NY*
Political Party: *Democratic*
Age at Inauguration: *47*
Served: *1885–1889*
Vice President: *Thomas A. Hendricks*

Grover Cleveland 1837–1908

Birthplace: *North Bend, OH*
Home State: *IN*
Political Party: *Republican*
Age at Inauguration: *55*
Served: *1889–1893*
Vice President: *Levi P. Morton*

Benjamin Harrison 1833–1901

Birthplace: *Caldwell, NJ*
Home State: *NY*
Political Party: *Democratic*
Age at Inauguration: *55*
Served: *1893–1897*
Vice President: *Adlai E. Stevenson*

Grover Cleveland 1837–1908

Birthplace: *Niles, OH*
Home State: *OH*
Political Party: *Republican*
Age at Inauguration: *54*
Served: *1897–1901*
Vice Presidents: *Garret A. Hobart, Theodore Roosevelt*

William McKinley 1843–1901

Birthplace: *New York, NY*
Home State: *NY*
Political Party: *Republican*
Age at Inauguration: *42*
Served: *1901–1909*
Vice President: *Charles W. Fairbanks*

Theodore Roosevelt 1858–1919

Birthplace: *Cincinnati, OH*
Home State: *OH*
Political Party: *Republican*
Age at Inauguration: *51*
Served: *1909–1913*
Vice President: *James S. Sherman*

William H. Taft 1857–1930

Woodrow Wilson 1856–1924

Birthplace: *Staunton, VA*
Home State: *NJ*
Political Party: *Democratic*
Age at Inauguration: *56*
Served: *1913–1921*
Vice President: *Thomas R. Marshall*

Warren G. Harding 1865–1923

Birthplace: *near Blooming Grove, OH*
Home State: *OH*
Political Party: *Republican*
Age at Inauguration: *55*
Served: *1921–1923*
Vice President: *Calvin Coolidge*

Calvin Coolidge 1872–1933

Birthplace: *Plymouth Notch, VT*
Home State: *MA*
Political Party: *Republican*
Age at Inauguration: *51*
Served: *1923–1929*
Vice President: *Charles G. Dawes*

Herbert Hoover 1874–1964

Birthplace: *West Branch, IA*
Home State: *CA*
Political Party: *Republican*
Age at Inauguration: *54*
Served: *1929–1933*
Vice President: *Charles Curtis*

Franklin D. Roosevelt 1882–1945

Birthplace: *Hyde Park, NY*
Home State: *NY*
Political Party: *Democratic*
Age at Inauguration: *51*
Served: *1933–1945*
Vice Presidents: *John N. Garner, Henry A. Wallace, Harry S. Truman*

Harry S. Truman 1884–1972

Birthplace: *Lamar, MO*
Home State: *MO*
Political Party: *Democratic*
Age at Inauguration: *60*
Served: *1945–1953*
Vice President: *Alben W. Barkley*

Dwight D. Eisenhower 1890–1969

Birthplace: *Denison, TX*
Home State: *KS*
Political Party: *Republican*
Age at Inauguration: *62*
Served: *1953–1961*
Vice President: *Richard M. Nixon*

John F. Kennedy 1917–1963

Birthplace: *Brookline, MA*
Home State: *MA*
Political Party: *Democratic*
Age at Inauguration: *43*
Served: *1961–1963*
Vice President: *Lyndon B. Johnson*

Lyndon B. Johnson 1908–1973

Birthplace: *near Stonewall, TX*
Home State: *TX*
Political Party: *Democratic*
Age at Inauguration: *55*
Served: *1963–1969*
Vice President: *Hubert H. Humphrey*

Richard M. Nixon 1913–1994

Birthplace: *Yorba Linda, CA*
Home State: *CA*
Political Party: *Republican*
Age at Inauguration: *56*
Served: *1969–1974*
Vice Presidents: *Spiro T. Agnew, Gerald R. Ford*

Gerald R. Ford 1913–

Birthplace: *Omaha, NE*
Home State: *MI*
Political Party: *Republican*
Age at Inauguration: *61*
Served: *1974–1977*
Vice President: *Nelson A. Rockefeller*

Jimmy Carter 1924–

Birthplace: *Plains, GA*
Home State: *GA*
Political Party: *Democratic*
Age at Inauguration: *52*
Served: *1977–1981*
Vice President: *Walter F. Mondale*

Ronald W. Reagan 1911–

Birthplace: *Tampico, IL*
Home State: *CA*
Political Party: *Republican*
Age at Inauguration: *69*
Served: *1981–1989*
Vice President: *George H. W. Bush*

George H. W. Bush 1924–

Birthplace: *Milton, MA*
Home State: *TX*
Political Party: *Republican*
Age at Inauguration: *64*
Served: *1989–1993*
Vice President: *Dan Quayle*

William Clinton 1946–

Birthplace: *Hope, AR*
Home State: *AR*
Political Party: *Democratic*
Age at Inauguration: *46*
Served: *1993–*
Vice President: *Albert Gore*

Home State refers to the state of residence when elected.